Outplacement
Techniques

Outplacement Techniques

A Positive Approach to Terminating Employees

WILLIAM J. MORIN
LYLE YORKS

A DIVISION OF AMERICAN MANAGEMENT ASSOCIATIONS

190511

658.313
M 858

Library of Congress Cataloging in Publication Data

Morin, William J.
  Outplacement techniques.

  Includes index.
  1. Employees, Dismissal of. 2. Executives,
Dismissal of. I. Yorks, Lyle. II. Title.
HF5549.5.D55M67   658.3'13   81-15018
ISBN 0-8144-5579-4   AACR2

First Printing

Preface and

Acknowledgments

DRAKE BEAM MORIN, INC., BECAME INVOLVED in the problems of terminated executives during the early 1970s in response to requests from long-time clients. Aware that DBM had both trained psychological counselors and personnel specialists on its staff, clients would request help in planning for the termination interview and providing career counseling for the dismissed executive. By 1974 outplacement counseling had become an integral part of Drake Beam Morin's consulting services, with a staff of specialized professionals serving clients. This book draws on the experiences DBM consultants have had, and continue to have, on a daily basis.

For Bill Morin, developing this manuscript has been an opportunity to commit to paper a broad range of practical experiences in working with major corporations on the problems of termination. These experiences have ranged from working with terminated CEOs with annual salaries in excess of $200,000 to nonexempts; from individual cases to group terminations.

For Lyle Yorks, the book has been an opportunity to think through how Drake Beam Morin's outplacement division blends with the wide range of other human resource management provided by our general consulting group. Terminations do not take place in a vacuum. The practices, procedures, and skills involved can be, and should be, integrated into a company's philosophy of human resource management.

We have benefited from the resources made available by many of our colleagues in the firm. In particular, we are indebted to Jim Cabrera, who was influential in moving DBM into outplacement counseling; Bob Delargey, who, during his tenure in charge of the outplacement counseling division, contributed much to the organization of DBM's outplacement practice; and Neil Redford and Skip Stellfox, who have played important developmental and administrative roles. We have also benefited from the observations of Steve Morris, whose comments were insightful and, in one instance, resulted in the reorganization of an entire chapter. We thank Leo Duvall and Wendy Frattini, who, as research assistants at Eastern Connecticut State College, helped in collecting important data for the book. Special thanks to Ellen Giammona, whose patience in preparing the manuscript is greatly appreciated.

The cases presented in this book are based on real situations. Names and in some instances job titles have been changed to protect the people involved.

William Morin

Lyle Yorks

Contents

Introduction

TERMINATION IS A SUBJECT THAT HAS BEEN largely ignored in the personnel management literature. This neglect has been reflected in corporate policies. Although people are fired every day, most companies invest few resources in training managers in how to manage the termination process effectively. Corporate procedures are usually brief, offering little, if any, guidance. Essentially, termination has been treated as one of those unpleasant necessities of life that just aren't discussed in polite company. From the organization's perspective, a termination is seen as evidence of a corporate failure, something best put behind and forgotten.

The neglect of this aspect of personnel management has undoubtedly extracted a price from both individuals and their organizations. Dismissing someone from work is a high-stress event. The manager doing the termination experiences stress both during the preparation stage and after the termination has been completed. In our experience, most executives are apprehensive about the termination process. Is the subordinate being treated fairly? Can the decision to terminate be supported by objective data? How will the person react? These are but a few of the questions that plague managers prior to initiating a dismissal. Later, guilt and self-doubt may continue in the manager's mind as he attempts to justify the decision to himself.

Being dismissed is hardly less stressful on the person being fired, or on that person's family. Economic problems are coupled with psychological issues of pride, status, and one's feelings of personal competence. A family's reaction can range from hostility rooted in the threat to its life-style to confusion over how to be supportive without appearing condescending.

Stress is generated among the terminated person's former co-workers as well. How do they relate to the discharged person? What are the implications for their own futures? These questions frequently go unaddressed.

There are, of course, other issues associated with termination. Legal implications, economic costs, and the disruption of organizational activities have to be considered. On the other side of the coin, many managers simply avoid discharging their people, opting instead to keep nonperformers on the corporate payroll. This is a cost of a different sort that is also rooted in our neglect of termination policy.

Despite the enormous stress that can accompany a termination, and a myriad of other possible consequences as well, managers are generally ill prepared to deal with the process. It is this problem we will be addressing here.

This book is intended for the personnel manager concerned with establishing and maintaining effective company practices in the area of termination and any manager who is confronted with the problem of letting someone go. We have described both the policies and the skills that should characterize the termination process. There is no way to make terminations pleasant! It is possible, however, to make them effective and avoid unnecessary pain and confusion for all concerned. We hope this book makes a contribution toward attaining this goal.

Part I

TERMINATION: POLICIES AND PRACTICES

Part I will examine the termination practices that typify industry today and offer a framework for ensuring that corporate practices in this area are responsible and effective. Chapter 1 provides a description of termination practices as we often encounter them, along with a discussion of the consequences organizations face as a result of these practices.

Chapter 2 examines the necessity of termination from the standpoint of the organization.

The third chapter offers a framework for establishing effective termination practices, starting with issues of policy and continuing into the establishment of programs and procedures for translating policy into action. Our discussion applies to both exempt and nonexempt workers. However, much of the recent attention being given to corporate outplacement programs focuses on managerial and professional employees.

Chapter 4 speaks directly to the handling of dismissals of nonexempt employees.

1

A Look at Corporate Termination Practices

IT'S AN AWKWARD SUBJECT—EXECUTIVE TERMI-
nation. Although less inevitable, it is right up there with
death and taxes in terms of popularity of experience. Yet
more than 20 percent of all managers find themselves out of work
at some point in their careers. Furthermore, companies are increasingly willing to terminate managerial personnel as a part of
efforts to cut costs or toward strengthening their management
team. Administrative and production workers are also exposed to
dismissal frequently, either for cause or as a result of corporate
relocations or reorganization. Indeed, terminating a subordinate
is a task that sooner or later confronts almost every manager.

Despite the fact that termination is a pervasive fact of corporate life, until recently the subject has been largely ignored in the
personnel literature. Industrial relations textbooks devote considerable space to recruitment and selection policies, career development practices, manpower planning techniques, and disciplinary procedures. Termination, however, is rarely given a line,
much less a chapter, despite the fact that personnel specialists
frequently find themselves handling the termination of both ex-

empt and nonexempt personnel. The manager's manual of a large Fortune 500 consumer goods company devotes exactly one paragraph—five sentences—to the handling of terminations. Almost never do corporate-sponsored management training programs handle terminations. In more than ten years of designing and conducting management training programs for some of the world's largest corporations, only once have we been requested to include the topic as part of a general management development program.

Yet it is a mistake to conclude that termination policies and skills are not very important. In interviews, managers report that firing someone is the most difficult thing they have to do. Few look forward to the task. Most procrastinate until they are forced to confront the issue; then they botch the process. As we will discuss shortly, the consequences for all involved—the company, the manager, and the person being terminated—can be formidable.

Few firms do a good job of managing the termination process. Consider the following two situations selected from hundreds of termination cases in our files.

BILL AND JOE

It is three o'clock on a Friday afternoon. Bill Ford, the department manager, has decided to terminate Joe Stepkowsky, his production manager. Bill comes from the school of management practice that holds that you have to tell people exactly where they stand. He has never been known to mince words. Joe has been with the company for ten years and has been production manager for two.

Bill is going to fire Joe because of the morale problems he has created in his department. Joe's peers consider him to be a problem, and they frequently complain to Bill that Joe is not performing. Last week, a couple of Joe's supervisors complained that they do not get any support from him. In short, Bill perceives that people don't like Joe and he is not part of the team.

Bill decided he had enough of these problems. He talked to his management, who agreed that Joe should be dismissed. Bill then went to personnel, had a benefits letter written up, and otherwise obtained personnel's support on the termination.

Joe is called off the shift and into Bill's office. Bill tells him to sit down and says: "I have something to tell you that is not very good news. I hope this doesn't come as a shock, but things are not working out and we are going to have to let you go."

Joe reacts with shock, asking Bill what he means by "let go." Bill tells him that his career with the company is over. Joe states that Bill cannot do this to him. Bill replies flatly that Joe's shift is clearly not working right. The morale problems are pretty heavy and there have been a lot of complaints about Joe's performance. He says "Even your overall attitude is poor."

Joe responds by stating that Bill never told him anything about his attitude or about being displeased with his performance. A year ago, Bill had talked with him about some morale problems on the shift, but never about his attitude. Bill responds by stating that Joe's last performance appraisal wasn't very good, and he should have seen the writing on the wall. Joe yells that his performance appraisal was average and his technical skills were rated very high.

Bill says, "Look, you knew there were problems in other areas."

Joe   You can't do this to me, Bill. I mean, I have worked here for ten years. You can't just come up and wipe me out with the back of your hand.

Bill   Well, look, I'm telling you—you're fired. I can't make it any clearer than that. You are not performing well.

Joe   I didn't know I wasn't performing; give me some examples.

Bill   Everybody on your shift says you are not cooperative. You are not leading them; the people don't even support you.

Joe   Well, that isn't true! I was just talking to some of the people the other night and they thought I was doing a super job . . . a much better job than six months ago.

Bill   Look, I am telling you to get out of here because you are through as of today. This letter describes your severance arrangements. The company supports this decision, so you better leave. We'll mail your things.

Stunned, Joe leaves the plant.

FRANK AND HARRY

Frank is a department manager. Sixty-one years old, he has been with the company for 23 years and in his current job for ten. He is popular and well liked by everyone, including his management. He generally gets the job done in his department.

Harry, one of his supervisors, has again missed his production schedule. This has been happening on and off for a year and a half, and management has told Frank he must terminate Harry. There are to be no more excuses; Harry must be fired.

Frank calls Harry into the office and the early conversation goes like this:

Frank   Would you like a cup of coffee? I don't know how to . . . uh . . . how is it going out there on the line?

Harry   It is going well. I'm sorry I missed my production schedule last month, but I'm getting it together.

Frank   Gee, we've talked about that before, haven't we, Harry? That you're going to get it together?

Harry   Yes, but I've been working on it. You know I have to put up with Mary out there. She's really been causing a lot of problems, but I talked to her the other night. I think we got our problem resolved.

Frank   Well, Harry, didn't we talk about Mary and her problem before? We've been talking about this for some time.

This scenario goes on for approximately two and a half hours and through three cups of coffee. Finally, Harry ends up by saying: "Well, you know, Frank, I've really enjoyed working with you all these years. Thank God you are going to give me another chance."

Frank answers with, "Now look, I am not really going to give you another chance, Harry. I want you to talk to personnel because I am going to have to take you off the shift in a couple of weeks—maybe a month. We are going to try to find you another job in the company."

Harry leaves, thanking Frank for this opportunity. He is wondering in what part of the company his new job will be located.

Aside from the question of whether either man's career with his company could have been salvaged, which of the two managers did a better job?

Neither did a good job. In fact, each botched the termination interview in a manner that was likely to make the consequences of the dismissal more difficult for both the company and the subordinate.

Bill destroyed Joe. He made it a group firing, blaming everyone else ("The people don't even support you."). He wanted Joe out, but he gave no substantial reasons, alluding only to vague issues. There was no dialogue. Discussion was all one way, with Bill telling Joe to get out but not telling him why.

Also, his timing (late on a Friday afternoon) compounded the problem. Joe was left to go home to a long weekend, not sure why he was fired and suddenly cut loose from his employer of ten years. Not the least of his problems was what to tell his family and fellow workers. Where does he go Monday morning? Joe's dismissal has all the markings of a brutal firing, which is how some of his colleagues at the plant are likely to view it.

Harry's case is no better, perhaps even worse. Harry doesn't know he is fired. His boss, Frank, beat around the bush and Harry manipulated the conversation. Harry is not focusing on the fact that he is losing his job on the shift, but that his boss is going to help him find another job in the company.

Frank has confused the issue by suggesting that Harry talk with personnel, and Harry believes he is being reassigned, not fired. He is in for a shock, of course. Frank is hoping personnel will do his job for him.

Neither Joe nor Harry has any realistic clue as to what went wrong on the job. Why did Bill and Frank make all these mistakes? Several factors contributed to the termination problems. However, two overriding causes in both these cases and others like them are:

1. *Lack of specific company policies for handling terminations.* In both instances, the companies had almost nonexistent policies beyond a statement to the effect that the supervisor should have job-related reasons for terminating a subordinate, and the termination should be approved by the boss's immediate superior. No further guidance was offered. No emphasis was given to the termination process.

2. *Lack of skill in handling terminations.* Neither Bill nor Frank had any idea of how a manager should approach a termination. Both were left to improvise. This was evident later on when, during interviews, both managers admitted they were unhappy with how the termination interview had gone. However, they did not know how to improve their performance. They were just aware that during the interview things had gone awry.

Typical Handling of Terminations

You may believe the two cases are exaggerated, but each is based on an actual situation. Furthermore, neither one represents an extreme handling of a termination. Outplacement specialists regularly see similar instances.

Historically, the most common corporate policy has been no policy. Some corporate war stories have become legendary.

There are executives who fire people by calling them in, asking for their keys, and having security escort them to the street. One large corporation simply transfers executives to dead-end jobs in the field and forgets about them. Gradually, they leave or retire. Hourly employees are easier to dismiss. A notice—the infamous pink slip—in the pay envelope solves the problem.

Such stories aside, what are the termination practices of large corporations? Systematic and reliable studies are almost nonexistent. A review of 1,200 actual terminations revealed the following patterns:[1]

- Most often the manager fires the subordinate after obtaining approval from his immediate superior. However, the actual termination interview varies greatly from manager to manager with little corporate guidance.
- Some people are fired so vaguely with so many euphemisms that they don't know they are being let go. Examples include, as in the case of Frank and Harry, promises of help in finding another job. Some people are told they would do well to think about other career choices, or they should closely examine how things are going on the job. Still others are told that the boss feels they have been working too hard and need a breather. Therefore, some of their key projects and responsibilities are being assigned to others. In these cases, the manager is hoping that the person will get the message.
- Still other terminated people are treated with excessive cruelty. Their personalities are attacked and they are charged with being incapable of handling responsibility, or they are subjected to the boss yelling at them and escorting them out of the office. Some are even fired over the phone. In one case a person was fired while ill in the hospital.

[1] A review of outplacement cases handled by Drake Beam Morin, Inc. These were people whose use of the outplacement services was sponsored by their former employers.

- Most terminations happen on Friday afternoon, with the fired person given little or no guidance about what to do next.
- The support packages offered each terminated employee vary widely. One might be given use of the office for several months, while another may be escorted to the street immediately.

Within one company, the variation of personal experience was remarkable. Of 21 managers who were let go within a 12-month period, four were ushered out of the building right after they had been terminated; several were allowed to clean out their desks but were told to be gone by the end of the day; five were given access to their offices for up to three months; three were given offices in another part of the building; and one had to vacate his office immediately but was permitted to have his former secretary take messages for him for 60 days.

The management manuals of ten Fortune 500 companies were essentially the same; a few paragraphs provided only superficial guidance for the handling of terminations. Basically, they were statements of corporate policy in the abstract, not descriptions of managerial procedure. Admittedly, ten companies is a limited sample. However, all ten were organizations known for their advanced management practices.

Historically this casual attitude has been reinforced by the courts. Writing in the *Harvard Business Review,* Clyde Summers notes that common law basically holds that an employer can dismiss an employee with or without good reason.[2] Summers cites the following cases as being illustrative of the attitude of the courts:

- A salesman for a steel corporation with 14 years of service was discharged after informing the vice-president in charge of sales that certain steel tubes were dangerous. The com-

[2]Clyde W. Summers, "Protecting All Employees Against Unjust Dismissal," *Harvard Business Review* (January–February 1980).

pany withdrew the tubes, but fired the salesman. The Pennsylvania Supreme Court supported the company's position, stating: "The law has taken for granted the power of either party to terminate an employment relationship for any or no reason."

- A secretary who was fired for reporting her availability for jury duty on the advice of a senior partner of her firm, but against the instructions of her supervisor, heard a California court declare: "Her employer could discharge her with or without cause. It makes no difference if the employer had a bad motive in doing so."
- The Louisiana Court of Appeals declared that a foreman was "an employee at will" and could be discharged at any time without notice.

In the absence of a written employment contract, court decisions have, with few exceptions, favored the employer. Recently a Michigan court ruled, however, that when an employer hires a person with the understanding that he is being retained for an indefinite period and can be terminated only for good cause, that understanding can be enforced. The court held that verbal assurances given during the recruitment process by company officials may be binding. So may statements of company policy or other company literature. It is too soon to judge whether this ruling is likely to be representative of a shift in judicial rulings. At least in Michigan, employers have to be concerned that company procedures are followed during terminations.

Historically, however, with the exception of those covered by labor agreements providing for arbitration rights or by written employment contracts, people have been without substantial protection from being terminated.

In recent years, civil rights legislation has extended protection to certain groups of people. Although the emphasis given by both government and management has been on discrimination in employment and promotion practices, the legislation applies to dismissal as well. Under federal law employers cannot discharge an employee *because* of that person's race, color, religion, sex, national origin, or age. This legislation has placed limitations on the arbitrary nature of termination decisions so far as members of protected classes are concerned.

Because of the possibility of charges of discrimination, companies have begun to be more thorough and deliberative when the person being considered for discharge is a woman, a member of a racial minority, or over 40 years old. However, this concern has tended to be highly uneven and on a case-by-case basis. Companies frequently scramble to assemble documentation after a complaint is filed, collecting data that should have been weighed before the decision was made.

Consequences of Poor Termination Policy

The available evidence suggests that severance policy has not been a high priority for management. Given the historical attitude of the courts, it is easy to see why. Still, contemporary organizations pay a price for poor termination policies; we believe that price justifies taking another look at how people are dismissed.

Economic Consequences

Poorly conceived severance policies may unnecessarily add to the cost of terminating a manager. To state the matter quite simply, most companies end up spending more on severance than is necessary. Often, a middle- or senior-level manager will leave with a year's severance pay, paid in one lump sum at the time of termination.

Under such an arrangement, a $50,000-a-year executive who is fired will cost a company $50,000 plus benefits. If the executive receives his severance pay at periodic intervals until he or she finds a new job, the economics are different. For example, if that same executive finds a job within four to six months, as many do when the termination is properly handled, the cost can be as little as $28,000 (including administrative costs associated with the termination)—a savings of almost 50 percent.

Other companies permit a terminated manager to remain on the job for up to six months handling many of his or her traditional responsibilities. During this time, the person receives full salary and benefits. However, experience indicates that under such an arrangement the manager tends to stay on for the full six months and leaves without having even identified potential employment contacts. Other managers who are more effectively terminated find employment in less than six months, again often saving thousands of dollars in salary and benefits.

Of course, when an executive exhausts his or her severance benefits, the consequences for the manager's personal finances can be devastating. Yet poor termination policies often encourage such a situation. The manager simply hangs around, expecting or hoping the company will have a change of heart.

Beyond the direct cost of terminations, poor policies typically lead to managerial shelf-sitters, who are a hidden cost to the company. The term "shelf-sitter" is most often used to describe the manager who is no longer considered a viable candidate for future development and/or promotion but is kept on the payroll. His performance in his present job is, at best, marginal. Most likely, he is not counted on to exercise real managerial responsibility.

No one is sure of the extent of shelf-sitters in American industry. Most informed observers agree that the trend from the 1960s into the 1980s has been for a significant increase in their number. Experts agree that the phenomenon is widespread.[3]

One large manufacturing and engineering company was recently advised by a major management consulting firm that close to a 50 percent reduction in managerial staff was appropriate. The

[3]Samuel R. Conner and John S. Fielden, "Rx for Managerial Shelf-Sitters," *Harvard Business Review* (November–December 1973).

company decided on a 25 percent cutback—a majority of whom were shelf-sitters. Similarly, a large New York insurance company recently found itself in the position of having to terminate a large number of employees, both exempt and nonexempt. Again, many of these people were shelf-sitters. In both firms, the cost of carrying these people for as many as ten years was formidable, so formidable that the companies were compelled to clean house in a particularly sudden and sweeping fashion.

Staff cutbacks such as the above are made necessary by more than shelf-sitting. Corporate relocations, new product mixes, new technology, and changing economic conditions are other factors that lead to group cutbacks. However, the practice of putting people aside when their performance indicates they must be replaced has added significantly to the administrative costs of many large companies, as organization consultants are painfully aware. Eventually, the difficult decisions have to be made. It is clear that in a period of low productivity and rising administrative costs, corporate tenure is going to be less and less tenable in American business. Termination is going to be a more frequent experience for managers and nonmanagers alike.

Psychological Consequences

The psychological consequences of a poor termination can be formidable both for the person being dismissed and for the manager who is doing the firing.

Much has been written in recent years about the relationship between a person's self-esteem and work. We are a society that assigns status according to a person's job. As noted by the special HEW task force on work in America: "In industrial America, the father's occupation has been the major determinant of status which in turn has determined the family's class standing, where they lived, where the children went to school and with whom the family associates . . . in short, the lifestyle and life chances of all family members."[4] With the emergence of women into the mainstream of management and other work roles, family class standing is increasingly becoming codetermined by the male's and/or female's occupation.

"On a more fundamental level, to be employed is to have daily evidence of one's worth to others. Diversely, not to have a job is not to have something that is valued by one's fellow human beings."[5] As Erich Fromm has observed: "In our society success or failure at work is seen as a direct measure of a person's value as a human being."[6]

This is reflected in the pragmatic problems that confront a terminated executive. Outplacement counselors report that nearly half of the managers with whom they work encounter accusations of failure rather than support from their immediate family.

"What are we going to do about the mortgage?"

"We can't take Billy out of school because you screwed up."

"You never do anything right."

These statements are indicative of the kinds of responses that can meet the manager at home. Suddenly, the manager's friends and acquaintances are too busy to see him. The terminated manager himself feels guilty, so much so that even when family and friends are supportive, he withdraws. His wife finds herself unsure of what reaction is appropriate.

The manager who finds himself without a job is faced with a number of confusing practical problems:

1. How do you prepare a résumé?
2. How do you get this résumé into the right hands instead of into the wastebasket?
3. How do you find out about potential jobs?

[4]*Work in America.* Report of a special task force to the Secretary of Health, Education and Welfare (Cambridge, Mass.: The M.I.T. Press).
[5]*Ibid.*
[6]Erich Fromm, *The Revolution of Hope* (New York: Harper & Row, 1964).

4. What do you tell associates?
5. What kinds of references will you get?
6. How do you answer when a potential employer asks why you were let go from your last job?

Consultants who specialize in working with terminated managers find that their clients are typically at a loss when trying to answer these kinds of practical questions. The problem has never come up before, or at least not recently.

Even with the best support, looking for a job can be one of life's most frustrating experiences. In the beginning, rejections and disappointments seem to outnumber successes. After only a week or two, it is easy to wonder "whether anybody wants me." No wonder songwriter Paul Williams writes: "The only thing worse than getting up for work is being unemployed."

The termination process can be traumatic for the executive doing the firing as well. By an overwhelming margin, most managers seek to avoid firing a subordinate. This is a major reason for shelf-sitting; it avoids the need to fire the person. Even managers who terminate with some directness usually experience some guilt over the process. A lack of clear-cut direction on how to handle terminations intensifies such feelings, leading to false starts and poorly handled confrontations. Months after a manager is terminated, his boss may still be trying to rationalize his actions. In fact, most outplacement consultants readily admit that the need to relieve the corporate conscience is a major reason for the rapid growth in the practice of providing counseling to terminated managers.

Organizational Consequences

The economic and psychological problems described above can be characterized as organization costs. There are, however, other consequences as well to the organization. A history of awkward terminations becomes known on college campuses and in recruiting circles. This is especially true at the better business schools. Corporate recruiters and campus placement directors are sensitive to the changing reputations of certain corporations.

One recruiter from a large corporation put the matter succinctly:

> We have had a difficult couple of years attracting top graduates. In the past, we have gone through cycles, recruiting heavily for a year or two and then leveling off and letting people go. Sometimes we ended up terminating people we had only recently recruited; other times, we were turning over experienced managers. In either case, it wasn't done with much finesse. Students today are sophisticated. They keep up with what is happening. It's amazing how often an attractive candidate asks about our pattern of letting people go. Who knows about the ones who don't sign up to interview?

The problem is more severe when recruiting experienced executives. The same recruiter commented: "We lost two preferred candidates for a senior-level position once the search firm identified us. Both bowed out graciously. We ended up talking with our third choice. We are going to have to live down our reputation for hatchet jobs on people."

When a senior manager is let go, he may begin to talk, and his comments can get into the business press. A manager may end up saying things about his former company that are better left unsaid. The comments may not even be true. On the other hand, is the company going to sue for libel? Probably not. The more poorly handled the dismissal, the more likely the grapevine is to pick up on the horror story.

Finally, an important consideration is the reaction of the terminated manager's peers and associates. If they perceive the manager as a victim who has been treated unfairly, morale can plummet and turnover increase. "What does the future hold for me?" and "Should I be looking elsewhere in self-defense?" are typical reactions among employees who have worked closely with a terminated manager.

At the nonexempt level, dismissals that are viewed as arbitrary and unfair contribute to a climate that is favorable to union organizing efforts. The protection afforded by arbitration rights in a collective bargaining agreement is an important argument of the organizer. It is so important to organizing efforts that unions have argued against legislation extending arbitration rights to all workers, fearing an adverse effect on their organizing activities. At a time when many companies feel that enlightened personnel policies can persuade employees that they will be treated fairly without resorting to a union, terminating practices are an important aspect of industrial relations.

Earlier we noted the negative impact poor termination practices can have on recruiting managerial and professional personnel. The same problems exist at the nonexempt level. Local plant and office personnel managers are aware that word-of-mouth communication from employees is an important recruiting device. Poorly handled severance of nonexempts can create a bad reputation in the community, disrupting the employment grapevine.

When members of protected classes under EEO legislation are involved, lawsuits can mean direct financial consequences as well. Worse, lack of a clear policy supported by supervisory training can lead supervisors to believe protected workers cannot be terminated. Thus, they tolerate behavior that undercuts control of the work unit. This is unfortunate, since it is simply not true that members of protected classes cannot be terminated. They just cannot be terminated in a discriminatory fashion, a distinction many supervisors don't understand.

A Growing Awareness of Outplacement

In recent years, a variety of labels have been used to describe the termination process—dehiring, derecruiting, outplacement, executive recycling, and the like. This terminology is more than cosmetic in nature; it represents a growing recognition of the stake a firm has in its termination practices. More importantly, companies are realizing that termination is something that can be managed; the consequences discussed above can be and should be controlled. Thus, the neglect of termination practices is beginning to be reversed.

This trend has started at the managerial level. Since the late 1960s, a growing number of firms have become aware of the value of providing systematic help to executives who are being dismissed. Indeed, this awareness is reflected in the growth of a new area of management consulting, most commonly referred to as outplacement counseling. If current projections are accurate, in ten years outplacement counseling will be a $100-million-dollar consulting business.

The results of a recent statistical review attest to the effectiveness of these outplacement efforts.[7] Over a two-year period, several hundred terminated executives who were receiving formal outplacement counseling were specifically tracked for purposes of analysis. The results showed that within an average of four and a half months 71 percent of the managers who found employment accepted positions at significantly higher salaries than those they received at former positions.

More specifically:

1. The average age of the manager terminated was 45.
2. The salary range was from $25,000 to $250,000.
3. The median salary of the terminated manager was $51,000.
4. Only ten people accepted employment at a lower income than that at the time of termination.
5. Only 21 were placed at the same income.
6. Sixteen made career changes. (Most left corporate life to pursue their own businesses.)

[7] Donald Monaco, "Outplacement Counseling: State of the Art," unpublished working paper, Drake Beam Morin, Inc., 1979.

More importantly, trained counselors identified and dealt with a significant number (30 percent) of people who presented either behavioral or personality trait problems.

Would the managers in the above study have found similar positions at the same pay within the same time frame without this formal outplacement counseling? Probably not. Unfortunately, a meaningful control group does not exist.

However, these results are more favorable than the experiences generally observed by personnel specialists. The average time out of work for an executive in this salary range is considered to be over six months, and the odds of locating a job at a significantly higher salary are thought to be no better than 50:50. Apparently a structured professional outplacement service, whether it is conducted by internal staff or by external consultants, can make a difference in the subsequent experience of a manager who is being let go.

To date, the majority of outplacement efforts have targeted toward managerial jobs. However, restricting such concern solely to the more senior levels is a mistake. In fact, corporate policies should include all employees—exempt and nonexempt. As noted above, a poorly handled dismissal of a nonexempt person can have disruptive organizational consequences. Among such consequences are lower morale of other workers, a poor reputation in the community (the employment grapevine), and pressure for unionization.

This book provides both an understanding of the termination process and a workable framework for managing that process effectively. The emphasis is on management practice, with theory kept to a minimum.

However, effective practice needs the guidance of a practice theory—a framework that provides a realistic orientation for termination as a personnel management function. What are the conditions under which termination should be considered? What are the goals of a termination? What factors should constrain termination? We turn to these and similar issues in Chapter 2.

2

Termination as an Organization Development Process

ALTHOUGH FEW MANAGERS FEEL THIS WAY AT the time they are fired, the simple fact is that many executives can look back on their careers and say that getting fired was the best thing that ever happened to them. Depending on the person and the situation, being dismissed can create an environment that forces a person to examine what he has been doing with his career and how well he has been doing it. Often a person is blasted from complacency or comes to realize that his job and career had been stagnant for some time. However, poor termination practices greatly reduce the potential benefits.

All too typical is the case of Harry Morgan. Harry was effectively placed on the shelf eleven years ago at the age of 42. "After all," went the reasoning, "Harry joined us right out of school; he has given us the best years of his life. It has been almost 20 years. Keeping Harry on is the responsible thing to do." Since that time, Harry has been given makeshift work, special projects, and, much of the time, nothing to do.

Then the economy went into a deep recession. The company's ability to respond was hampered by, among other things, too much deadwood. Senior management found an attitude of complacency among people in many key customer service spots. As part of the corporate redevelopment plan, Harry, and others like him, would have to go. Budgets were being cut. Harry was a luxury the company could no longer afford.

Now Harry was 53 and out of work. Furthermore, he had not received a promotion in more than 13 years. Nor was he in a position to talk to a potential employer about any recent accomplishments. Not having been challenged in more than a decade, his approach to the job search process was timid and uncertain. In short, Harry was not an attractive job candidate. Corporate responsibility had backfired.

Replacing Managers for Organization Development

Replacing a manager is often a necessary method of organizational change, one that has been given short shrift in the voluminous literature on organization development. Porter, Lawler, and Hackman have noted that:

> Just as organizations can be changed by recruitment and selection practices, so also they can be changed by practices regarding who is encouraged or required to leave the organization . . . yet it is true that by systematically eliminating from an organization those individuals who cannot or consistently will not work effectively toward organizational goals, the overall level of organizational effectiveness often can be improved.[1]

They conclude that many times, in the long run, "the best interests of the organization and the employee are served by the individual not staying in a position to which he is not suited."

[1]Lyman W. Porter, Edward E. Lawler III, and J. Richard Hackman, *Behavior in Organizations* (New York: McGraw-Hill, 1975), p. 442.

Larry Greiner of the University of Southern California has observed as organizations grow they move through identifiable stages.[2] Moreover, as the organization moves from one stage to another, an atmosphere of considerable turmoil is often generated as the management styles, techniques, and structures that led to success in the previous stage prove problematical for the growing organization.

For example, in a very small organization a lack of formal managerial structure is appropriate. Informal communication between people in the organization helps foster a creative and entrepreneurial atmosphere. However, success leads to growth, and as the organization grows, the lack of structure leads to confusion and lack of direction. Gradually, a crisis is reached, during which the need for more centralized and formal systems becomes apparent. These changes are often difficult for many members of the firm to accept.

If the company is successful in establishing more formal and centralized policies and procedures, continued growth becomes possible. At some point, however, the organization finds itself becoming too rigid and inflexible to respond properly to changes in various areas of its increasingly complex environment. At this point a new crisis is generated, one that is usually resolved with the adoption of a decentralized form of management structure that emphasizes delegation of authority to division and middle managers. Eventually, this stage becomes unwieldy as well, as further growth forces the imposition of additional controls onto an increasingly diverse organization.

Greiner's analysis makes two points:

1. As organizations grow, they are forced to adopt forms of structure and management systems that are appropriate to their stage of development. Such adaptation is a prerequisite of continued growth.

[2]Larry E. Greiner, "Evaluation and Revolution as Organizations Grow," *Harvard Business Review* (July–August 1972).

2. With continued growth, management structures that permitted past growth to occur effectively will become obso-
   lete.

In other words, successful managerial methods often generate their own demise. The very growth that the methods helped
generate creates new conditions, for which new methods and
stuctures must be employed.

Consider the practical effects of Greiner's arguments for individual managers. Although many managers can adapt from the
informal structure of a small company to the more centralized
bureaucratic environment, company histories are replete with examples of senior managers, even founders, who have had to be
replaced in order for the proper management systems to be installed. An autocratic and structured manager may be highly effective at a certain point in a company's history; at another point
in time, his style will begin creating problems rather than solving
them. Similarly, a manager whose delegation skills have been
critical to the success of the company to date might find these
same skills counterproductive as the organization evolves.

Managers caught in the middle of such organizational crises
are often confused when confronted with the reality that they are
not as effective as in the past. The manager may resist the new
managerial approaches being implemented in the organization as
a personal repudiation. Yet it is not that the manager is any less
skillful than before, but that his managerial strengths are no
longer appropriate to the new set of organizational problems his
past successes have helped generate. Somewhere else is an organization that may be floundering for lack of a manager with his
particular skills.

Appropriately, most organizations turn to training and development in an effort to help managers adapt. No doubt some
managers respond to this training and once more become meaningful contributors to the organization. The reality, however, is
that the occupational habits of a lifetime are hard to break. In
many cases, a significant amount of the training is not transferred

to the job, and the manager finds himself under increasing fire for his methods. Eventually, he is bypassed, finding himself outside the mainstream of the company for which he was once a meaningful performer. Worse, the manager may remain in a key position, hindering rather than helping the organization's progress.

Fred Fiedler has presented data on how difficult it is to change a manager's style.[3] He concludes that at times it might be simpler to design the job around the manager than to try to adapt a manager's style to fit a particular situation. Unfortunately, this is a solution of limited application.

Humanistic Psychology and Management Development

The impact of humanistic psychology on management development programs is seen in the emphasis placed on personal growth in managers. Throughout the 1960s and 1970s, most training and development specialists subscribed to theories in the tradition of writers such as Abraham Maslow, Douglas McGregor, Chris Argyris, Warren Bennis, and Robert Blake and Jane Mouton. Although each of their theories is associated with different organization development techniques, they all share a common belief in the responsiveness of most managers to organizational structures that encourage a fuller utilization of their abilities. The cumulative effect of their collective influence has been an industrial human potential movement in management development.

A considerable body of literature on developing effective managerial and leadership skills has evolved—much of it by writers steeped in the humanistic tradition. This literature offers a number of techniques for altering the managerial style of practicing managers. Ranging from interpersonal competence labs to survey feedback methods to human relations training, these tech-

---

[3]Fred E. Fiedler, *A Theory of Leadership Effectiveness* (New York: McGraw-Hill, 1967).

niques all attempt to improve managerial effectiveness by altering the manager's behavior on the job. Generally, the intended nature of the style change aims at getting the manager to:

1. Demonstrate trust and confidence in the ability of subordinates to achieve high performance goals.
2. Listen to and utilize the ideas of subordinates when engaged in problem-solving activities.
3. See that subordinates are well trained and otherwise receive support for their efforts.

This humanistic approach asserts that organizations that evolve into open, organic structures tend to be more effective than those that are autocratic and mechanistic. However, the weight of existing evidence supports a more complex theory of organization management.

Paul Lawrence and Jay Lorsch have presented extensive data that suggest that although open, organic, and participative organizations are highly effective in turbulent, rapidly changing market conditions, such organizations are less effective in very stable environments than more bureaucratic, centralized, and autocratic companies.[4] Burns and Stalker, Lorsch and Morse, and Richard Hall have also presented evidence in support of this view.[5-7] Indeed, the above studies are at the heart of the so-called contingency approach to management currently popular in business schools.

At a minimum, these studies support the view that under differing environmental conditions, certain managerial styles are

[4]Paul F. Lawrence and Jay W. Lorsch, *Organization and Environment: Managing Differentiation and Integration* (Homewood, Ill.: Richard D. Irwin, Inc., 1969).

[5]Tom Burns and G. S. Stalker, *The Management of Innovation* (London: Tavistock Publications, 1961).

[6]J. W. Lorsch and J. J. Morse, *Organizations and Their Members: A Contingency Approach* (New York: Harper & Row, 1974).

[7]Richard H. Hall, "Intraorganizational Structure Variation," *Administrative Science Quarterly* (December 1962).

more effective than others. Couple this research to the possibility that many managers will simply find that modifying their style in response to changing organizational conditions is an unrealistic task, and termination becomes a legitimate method for furthering the development of both the organization and the careers of individual managers.

There are other compelling reasons for terminating someone. The most important is that a manager is no longer performing, regardless of the organization's stage of growth or environment. If, for whatever reason, a person has been promoted to a job level beyond his or her capacities, often only the shock of being let go will initiate the kind of self-assessment that is likely to generate more realistic career aspirations. Of course, for a termination to accomplish this, you need support far beyond our traditional approaches of discharging people.

Utilizing Human Resources

In the mid-1960s, the behavioral science school of management theory began to differentiate between traditional human relations in management and a new alternative: the human resource model.[8] Human relations practices, went the argument, emphasized treating people better, but it overlooked the issue of utilizing them well.

The new perspective of the human resource model argued that people are an economic resource that requires full utilization if they are to maximize their performance potential. Some writers have suggested that human resources should be audited, much like the financial and capital resources of the corporation.[9] This

[8]Raymond Miles, "Human Relations or Human Resources," *Harvard Business Review* (July–August 1965).
[9]Rensis Likert and D. G. Bowers, "Organizational Theory and Human Resources Accounting," *American Psychologist* (June 1969).

reasoning is based on the premise that such human resource accounting practices would require management to pay more attention to the state of the firm's human assets.

The emergence of the human resource perspective has been a watershed event in the history of personnel management. It has clearly marked the crucial charcteristics that separate paternalism from the genuine development of people. In so doing, it carries some interesting implications for termination policy.

Although the history of the human resource model has been to focus attention on the training, development, and utilization of people, it also provides a rationale for management assessing people carefully and terminating those who cannot meet or are not meeting the organization's needs. When organizational conditions change, preserving or redeploying people is often problematic. And, as the human resource model makes clear, in the long run paternalism is often destructive to the individual.

However, human resources are different from other resources in a most important sense—people have both a need for and a right to individual dignity. People are neither extensions of nor analogous to machines. The history of management practices demonstrates that any approach to managing that attempts to deal with people as though this were not true is doomed to eventual failure. Ultimately, other resources can simply be scrapped; employees expect and deserve more. Terminations should be handled according to policies that strive to avoid degrading the value of the human resource.

We are not suggesting that terminating an employee is something managers should look forward to doing with great frequency. Indeed, termination often represents failure of other management systems. However, given our form of industrial organization, the need for periodic dismissals is a fact of life. Our argument is for the recognition of the need for periodic dismissals and for the development of policies that will manage the process effectively.

Effective Manpower Management: Minimizing the Need for Termination

Termination is not the primary method of changing organizations. Although it is often a necessary method of change, it isn't a desirable one. A high termination rate is generally an indicator that other personnel management systems are not operating effectively. Before examining some of these other systems, however, it will be helpful to analyze why people are fired.

The Causes of Termination

In analyzing the reasons for termination in cases handled by our firm over the last six years, a definite pattern emerges. At the lower levels of the organization (nonexempt administrative personnel, first-line supervisors), competency is a dominant reason. However, at the management level, the reason for firing someone is likely to be related to personality conflicts with the boss.

Although the files seldom explicitly stated the matter, nearly 80 percent of managerial terminations were traceable to personality-related conflicts between boss and subordinate. The corporate personnel managers we interviewed supported this conclusion, stating that in the majority of instances, managers are fired because they can't integrate themselves into the boss's "way of doing things."

In other words, it is the inability of managers to fit into a given organizational setting in which the boss is comfortable that generates problems in *personal* effectiveness. Most often, the disagreement is over how the job should be done. At the root of these differences are the attitudes, traits, and personal styles of the people involved.

Occasionally we encounter a person with a style so extreme that he runs through a number of jobs in different companies. Such cases require professional counseling. More typically, a clash with a specific boss results in the individual being let go, although he may have functioned very well in the past. As one manager expressed it: "You work for one guy, you are a hero; another tells you you are a bum; on the next job, you are a hero again."

In our experience, corporate reorganizations or cutbacks account for another 8 to 10 percent of terminations. This figure is higher at the lower job levels. Here, the manager is often caught in a series of circumstances beyond his control. Some effective executives find their jobs eliminated due to changing circumstances. Some have even worked themselves out of a job.

Pure job incompetence explains less than 5 percent of terminations we handled at the managerial level. Included here are the shelf-sitters who are labeled as ineffective and continually passed over for promotion. Incompetence does not always lead to immediate dismissal. When the subordinate is easy to get along with, or has "been on the team," the first response of the boss is to protect him. The subordinate is given a noncritical job and placed on the shelf. It is when the subordinate clashes with his superior that incompetence leads to rapid consideration of termination as a solution. Thus, personality can affect the dismissal of even an incompetent subordinate.

Incompetence is, of course, relative. To be incompetent at one job does not mean you are unemployable. In another job, with other responsibilities, the same person might prove quite capable.

What does the above discussion imply for a company's manpower planning systems? Termination is only one of the control points at which an organization can control its employment mix. Let's examine some of the others.

Recruitment and Termination

A systematic analysis of a company's termination patterns often suggests the need for improvement in recruiting practices.

If a firm takes a hard, realistic look at why it ends up dismissing people, it often becomes clear that many problems can be headed off during the employment selection process. In our own experience, analysis of client organizations has frequently revealed that too often inadequate attention was given to the personal style of a potential applicant and how he and his future boss might function together.

James C. Cabrera, a consultant experienced in both recruiting and outplacement, has observed that in recruiting key managers, too little attention is given to the personal chemistry between the new manager and his immediate superior. Cabrera suggests that in recruiting managers for an organization, considerable attention be given to the question of whether the two people can work together.

Is one detail-orientated, and the other more impatient and decisive? What if one is creative and innovative and the other is more cautious in his thinking? Although such differences do not always forecast interpersonal conflicts, it is reasonable to make them explicit before offering employment to an applicant. It requires a mature manager to tolerate significant differences in personality in a subordinate and to view these differences as compensating for one's own blind spots.

Cabrera recommends that the recruitment manager give careful consideration to the personal characteristics that the boss thinks are important to success in the job before the search is initiated. What kind of environment does the boss create for his subordinates? Is it highly structured, with close supervision, or does the boss give subordinates considerable autonomy? How much emphasis does the boss place on personal organization and adherence to formal procedures in carrying out work assignments? How does the boss make decisions? Does he prefer to be presented with a subordinate's best recommendation or does he like to examine all the options personally?

Such data, collected through interviews with the boss and his subordinates, can be translated into specific characteristics that the successful applicant should have. These characteristics should then be explored with the boss, and his reaction obtained. It is important that the characteristics specified be limited to those few that experience clearly indicates are important to the level of effectiveness between this particular executive and his subordinates. These should be discussed frankly before the search process begins.

Unfortunately, such an analysis doesn't always precede a job search, so that an applicant might be selected who does not have the temperament for performing well in his new environment. Two or three years later the recruit finds himself a candidate for dismissal.

Future-Oriented Job Specifications

Job specifications should be oriented to the future, not the past. Industrial psychologist John Drake notes that frequently a recruiter relies heavily on past managers as models in developing job specifications.[10] People who were successful in the job over the past five or ten years are not necessarily good models for future success. This is especially true when the organization is undergoing rapid changes. When developing job specifications, a corporate recruiter should focus on (a) the current demands of the job in question and (b) anticipated future demands.

How does the boss see the job evolving? Where will the incumbent manager be expected to move, both while in the job and in terms of long-range development? What new skills will be required of the person holding down the position? Conscious consideration of questions such as these can help avoid unnecessary terminations; attention should be focused during the recruitment process on characteristics that are required if the person is to grow with the company.

[10]John D. Drake, *Interviewing for Managers* (New York: AMACOM, 1972).

A considerable body of literature exists on recruitment and selection. Our intent in this book is neither to duplicate nor to supplement it. Suffice it to note that analysis of termination patterns often reveals weaknesses in a company's recruitment practices.

Stripped of the finer points, when hiring subordinates most managers are basically interested in whether the person has the technical ability to do the job they need done and whether they can work with this person. Failure on one or both of these points leads to termination.

Human Resource Planning

Beyond selecting the proper people for the organization, there is the matter of effectively planning the utilization of those employees who have been recruited. Analysis of an organization's termination patterns often reveals that people are terminated because the company failed to identify certain development needs early in their careers or, in other cases, has simply misassigned them.

Performance appraisal emerges as an important part of any human resource planning system. Properly managed, the appraisal process can help provide reasonably accurate assessments of a person's capabilities and development needs. Even more important, a well-conceived approach to appraisal helps avert problems before they become severe and aids in the development of employees.

Unfortunately, most organizations fail to maintain effective appraisals. All too often the appraisal becomes a tool for justifying salary decisions. Under such conditions, appraisals reflect more about what the company is willing to pay than the appraisee's actual performance, strengths, and weaknesses. Other times, the information on the appraisal is not transferred to a centralized human resource information system where it is readily available when staffing and training decisions are made.

A much underestimated device for managing an organization's human resource flow is the management inventory. Essentially, a management inventory is to a business what a depth chart is to an athletic team. Every year, key managers (division, plant, and department heads) complete the inventory on crucial managerial and administrative slots that report to them.

The incumbent of each slot is evaluated along several dimensions, usually:

Level of current performance
Level of qualifications for current performance
Level of anticipated future performance
Promotability

Successors to these positions are typically evaluated as well, with the manager often required to identify two or three possible backups for each slot, along with their degree of preparedness for assuming the job. Development plans for improving the preparedness of these successors are also required. This information is then integrated with a statement on how the manager expects his human resource requirements to change given present and future business plans. This information is reviewed with the person's superior and then fed into the centralized human resource information system.

A management inventory does not provide any automatic answers. When completed annually, however, the inventory imposes a rigor on the human resource planning process that comes with repeatedly asking the right questions. Individuals who have not made any progress or whose performance is slipping are likely to be identified at an early stage and targeted for corrective development action. Alternative career paths resulting from changed business objectives are likely to be illustrated by the inventory. Managers whose progress has stagnated can be highlighted in a timely fashion. In short, management inventories can help an organization stay on top of many career-path-related issues.

Of course, both appraisals and management inventories must be supplemented by an investment in management development training if the organization is to maximize its efforts to avoid unnecessary terminations.

Establishing and maintaining an effective human resource system is a topic beyond the scope of this book. A frequent need to resort to termination should, however, lead a company to audit its practices in this area.

Mid-Career Guidance

Although major organizations are increasingly examining their outplacement policies, few have seriously looked at mid-career guidance. In essence, mid-career guidance is evolving today as an effort to stave off termination. Remember, at managerial levels, a majority of people are terminated because of the chemistry that exists between them and their boss or other managers above them. Mid-career guidance can often help a person modify the behavior that is creating difficulties with the boss.

Often, if a person knows that he is doing certain things that are not acceptable to his manager, peers, or management, he will strive to change that aspect of his behavior. In essence, all the boss wants, many times, is a change in behavior, not a personality change.

For example, in one instance, we were asked to work with a manager whose job was in jeopardy because management was uncertain whether it could trust his judgment. In pressing this issue with his superiors, we found that the individual involved tended to hesitate when expressing his opinion on something, a trait others interpreted as indicating a lack of confidence in his opinion. Conversations with the manager revealed that he felt he was not really being asked for his opinion. He was unaware of how his behavior was being read by others.

Once he understood the problem, he worked to eliminate the hesitant behavior that communicated uncertainty instead of caution on his part. He also worked on skills that helped him to clarify his boss's expectations. Subsequently, his superiors came to view him as having "grown and developed more confidence." Less than a year after having received what we now call "mid-career guidance counseling," the manager was promoted to a more responsible position within his division.

This kind of development counseling often takes place between a boss and subordinate or comes from a mentor within the company. Sometimes, however, performance problems create a tension the boss finds difficult to overcome. Either the boss lacks the skills to counsel the subordinate effectively or the subordinate is too defensive toward his superior. In such situations, a third-party counselor can often provide the needed assistance that can help salvage a person's career for the company.

Simply helping to clarify expectations is a very meaningful role when one considers that today a company may have $500,000 to $1 million invested in an employee after 20 to 30 years of service. To fire such a person or say that he or she has "Peter principled" or "plateaued out" without first making an effort at turning that person's career around is to write off a significant investment. Replacement costs add to the expense of terminating a person.

It is our opinion that the poor quality of communication that characterizes many performance appraisal systems, coupled with a tendency for subordinates to claim they understand the feedback they are getting from a boss when, in fact, they do not, generates considerable waste in our utilization of people. There are a great many needless terminations today.

Simply put, mid-career guidance provides a third-party reference point in an effort to save a person's career with a given organization. This guidance can be oriented toward eliminating a specific problem, as in the illustration above, or it can be directed toward attempting to overcome a more general leveling in a person's performance pattern.

When Not Terminating Is a Mistake

Few things in life are as traumatic as being fired. It is our hope that the above discussion makes clear our belief that dismissal should be considered only when other human resource management approaches have not produced results. Managers should not expect termination to be a regular part of their job. In fact, an excessive termination rate is usually indicative of a deep-rooted managerial problem.

Nevertheless, as we have indicated above, there are times when termination is an appropriate managerial strategy. More specifically, such situations include:

Poor job performance. When an employee's work performance is unsatisfactory, and specific performance criteria have repeatedly been explained to the employee, failure to terminate is a mistake. The firm is not realizing a return on its investment in the person. Furthermore, someone else usually has to pick up the slack. In addition to imposing extra costs, this can generate a morale problem on the part of others, leading to more problems. The longer the poor performer is carried, the less management can expect other workers to be responsive to peformance standards.

Failure to comply with company regulations and rules. Included here is failure to comply with personnel regulations as well as any other set of established organization policies. For example, excessive absenteeism or tardiness that violates existing standards for a job classification must be dealt with and corrected to maintain management credibility. The same applies to any type of procedure. When an employee has been warned repeatedly that his or her behavior violates published standards and the person still refuses to comply, termination is a reasonable solution.

Blocking of a talented, ambitious middle manager's progress by a slightly more effective group of peers. This situation often emerges in large corporations that consistently recruit top managerial talent. A middle manager who is very capable consistently misses promotions because there are always one or two peers who are slightly better and more qualified for the slot. The end result is a manager whose career progress begins to stagnate.

It is often easy for both the corporation and the manager involved to lose sight of the fact that, despite his lack of current advancement, he is really competing against an extremely capable peer group and is still measuring up in a reasonably favorable light. In fact, he might be as capable of performing at a higher level of responsibility as those who have gotten promotions. There are certainly other companies for whom this person would prove an outstanding addition to the management team.

If the manager seems content with the situation and is doing his job effectively, it is in the best interest of the organization to retain him. However, if the person's ambitions are producing signs of discontent, it is best to address the issue frankly with that person. Under those conditions, the first option ought to be to sit down with the person and, through a career counseling process, help him see that perhaps his career opportunities would be better elsewhere.

The result of such counseling is often a voluntary termination. However, if such efforts fail and the manager clearly *remains ambitious and becomes increasingly discontented, resulting in declining job performance,* anything other than a nonvoluntary termination is a disservice to the manager as well as the company.

If the policy of a company is "up or out" to ensure continued development of managerial talent within the organization, immediate termination is advisable for a person who is not a serious candidate for advancement. The longer the company procrastinates, the more severe the consequences are likely to be for the individual involved.

Inability of a boss to deal· effectively with a subordinate. Whenever a boss feels he cannot manage a subordinate effectively and repeated corrective counseling does little or nothing to alleviate the situation, termination looms as the only workable solution. Failure to terminate someone who repeatedly performs below the boss's expectations and fails to respond to counseling represents a threat to the boss's ability to meet organization goals. At the nonexempt level, a serious disciplinary problem can emerge if other workers feel certain people are "getting away" with not performing.

Lack of relevance of a manager's strengths to the needs of the corporation. As discussed earlier in this chapter, organizations go through cycles. At different points in the organization's history, a different mix of managerial strengths and weaknesses is required. When it is clear that the strengths of a particular manager are no longer relevant to the needs of the organization and development of other skills, strengths, or management style is impractical or highly unlikely, procrastinating on the termination decision only serves to drag out an uncomfortable situation. This problem is almost always reflected in performance. The manager is unable to function effectively in the evolving environment.

These considerations highlight the developmental aspect of termination policy. Unfortunately, organizations often delay in addressing these issues within the context of development. For example, companies may invest thousands in training some highly authoritarian managers to delegate to and utilize subordinates more effectively, but to no avail. Years later these managers are still resisting change while the organization suffers. With the productivity demands of the 1980s, we feel companies will come to understand that outplacement is often the most effective solution.

As is the case with any set of considerations that are weighted prior to taking action, the termination rule should never be applied in any sort of mindless, bureaucratic, reactive fashion. In every instance termination should be preceded by either corrective or career-oriented counseling, and perhaps some alternative career counseling.

However, once it becomes clear that these strategies are not providing a meaningful solution, termination emerges as a viable, indeed necessary, vehicle for organizational change. Chapter 3 elaborates on the reasons for terminations and provides a practical framework for establishing corporate policy in this area.

3

Effective Corporate Termination Practices

HAVING SURVEYED HOW ORGANIZATIONS TYPically deal with terminations, the problems caused by poorly handled dismissals, and the reasons termination is often appropriate, we are left with a practical question: How can a company manage terminations effectively? The framework for termination practices offered in this chapter has emerged out of our experiences with a wide range of companies. The policies and procedures it contains reflect the backdrop of our previous discussion.

As with all organizational activities, consistency throughout a company in how terminations are handled requires a well-defined policy. In the absence of clearly articulated policy, termination practices will vary not only from division to division, but from department to department, and even within departments. The first step in establishing effective termination practices is for the senior corporate personnel officer to obtain top management agreement on several policy issues.

Foremost among these issues is specifying what constitutes

grounds for termination. Although most companies have policy statements on severance and involuntary termination, they are usually very general regarding the reasons for termination. Only vague guidance is offered to the manager.

Grounds for Termination

A corporate termination policy should state flatly that the company will not tolerate terminations supported by vague reasons. The policy must make it clear that managers have to document their case for termination with concrete business reasons.

Surprisingly, this is not often the case. Outplacement consultants find that in most cases the boss is very fuzzy about why an executive is being terminated. Frequently the reasons given are similar to:

"He is not on my team."

"I can't communicate with him any more."

"She didn't understand the new direction."

"He always seemed to be confused."

Hardly ever do consultants hear that the person failed to accomplish specific goals.

In reality, the terminated manager's performance has usually been marked by problems. Over a period of time, the person has been hurting his organization, but the company has tolerated his poor performance. All of a sudden, there is new management over the individual in question or an awakening on the part of the boss because his tolerance of the problem has gotten his department into trouble. A lot of things can change that suddenly bring about an awareness of the person's lack of performance. When the consultant traces the situation back in time, a true lack of performance typically emerges. However, management fails to articulate that lack of performance and instead gives its rationale for dismissal in vague, superficial terms.

Performance-Related Reasons

- Harry Johnson's department repeatedly has low efficiency ratings. For some time now, Harry has been unable to improve the situation, despite the urgings of his boss.
- Mary Wilson submits marketing plans which have consistently failed to demonstrate either increased sales or consumer awareness of the product.
- Fred Esco has not yet evaluated the impact of the message consumers will get in the advertising campaign for a new product introduction. The product introduction is only five weeks away. Fred is late on other deadlines as well.
- John Foster's people frequently violate personnel policies, creating a great deal of discontent in other departments. It appears that either John cannot or will not maintain discipline over his people.
- Diane Sauter has been rated poorly on several of her major projects. It is unlikely she will be promoted. Her firm operates on an "up or out" policy.

All five of these people represent the most justifiable of termination reasons—repeated poor work performance. Unfortunately, in each of the above cases, the company botched the termination badly. Documentation was shaky (although thorough investigation substantiated the performance problem), previously held performance counseling sessions were not well recorded, and there was some reason for the subordinate to believe management would be tolerant of the poor work for at least the near future. Making matters worse, the companies were planning to obscure the reasons for the discharge, in two instances trying to soften the blow with comments like "Things just didn't work out."

It is remarkable how often companies muddle up a termination even when strong evidence of poor performance exists.

Company policy should be directed toward avoiding mistakes such as the ones above.

When considering a performance-based termination, management should identify at least three solid reasons the individual should be terminated—for example, failure to reach certain agreed-upon objectives or repeated failure to meet specific job performance standards. Performance-oriented guidelines that should be included in corporate policy are:

Three consecutive below-average performance appraisals. In many instances companies don't have any poor appraisals on record at time of termination. This indicates that:

1. Companies tend to terminate on an emotional basis, and/or

2. Performance appraisals are not conducted properly.

Often the boss is reacting to a specific incident, the straw that broke the camel's back. "I don't like him. That's it. I've had it with him. He is going today." That is the reactive thought process of the supervisor. He calls in the subordinate and tells him he is not satisfied with his work and the company is not going to tolerate it any more. The boss has not thought out the specifics, nor are they documented anywhere.

Most likely the terminated person has gotten by with average performance appraisals. To the boss, however, average means below average; his better people are all rated either above average or outstanding. These ratings support his compensation and promotion decisions without causing unnecessary confrontations with the poor performer; confrontations, his experience tells him, will lead to increased tension on the job.

One consequence of this philosophy is that documentation for the termination decision is nonexistent. This seriously hurts the firm if equal employment opportunity litigation is started, since the courts base their decision on the contents of the appraisal file. Beyond the matter of legal defense is the fact that reviews that fail to document performance problems do not provide the person involved with a reasonably accurate picture of where he stands with his boss. Even when specific problems and conflicts have arisen on the job, the person is able to conclude that overall he is doing all right. A false sense of security is generated, setting the individual up for a real shock. Failure to provide comprehensive and thorough appraisals of poor performance shows a lack of managerial integrity. The manager who avoids giving such feedback is sidestepping his responsibility.

At least three missed performance objectives. Supplemental to the required documentation on the performance appraisals, a terminated person should be given at least three reasons for being fired. This helps him or her to digest what went wrong with the job. These reasons are best spelled out in terms of specific job objectives that were not completed.

Obviously, this policy is easier to implement when managerial and professional staff have their responsibilities expressed in results-oriented objectives on an annual basis. Even in the absence of a management-by-objectives program, however, corporate policy can specify that a terminated manager be given at least three reasons for the termination, and that these reasons be expressed in an objectives-oriented format, the objectives having been shared previously with the manager. Such a policy places pressure on managers who are thinking of terminating a subordinate to communicate specific job-related performance objectives before making the final termination decision.

Outplacement consultants find that when specific objectives have been clearly articulated, there is less conflct during the termination process. It is when the reasons given are vague ("I don't think you are doing too well in your job") that the person being terminated will argue. When there are specific failures that management can delineate, the terminated person may say, "I'm sorry you see it that way; I disagree with you. I think there were a lot of extenuating circumstances." But there is usually not a heated argument.

It is when the reasons are not specific that the person feels wronged and wants his day in court. He or she is not quite sure of the reason for the dismissal. Psychologically, a person needs to have three or four reasons why he or she is being terminated, in order to have something with which to assess what happened.

A rating of nonpromotable in a management development track job. Many companies have sophisticated management development programs that involve promotion and job rotation in order to evolve a strong group of generalistic managers for the business. Often labeled "fast-track programs," they are filled with young managers who are hired explicitly for development. In such companies it is generally understood that entry into middle- and senior-level managerial slots occurs solely through their management development programs.

A number of these programs are characterized by an up-or-out policy, especially at the lower levels. A person who does not appear to have the potential to advance will be encouraged (or required) to leave the company in order to keep the lines of advancement open for the next generation of managerial talent. Indeed, in some companies, such as the large accounting firms, almost all professional jobs are on an up-or-out basis. From the start, the need for continual advancement is understood by the employee.

When companies have explicit career ladders along which a manager or a professional person is expected to advance, a rating of nonpromotable should trigger consideration of the termination decision. Although the specifics will vary from situation to situation, policy should require that:

1. The length of time in grade before being assessed for promotion be spelled out for each job. In most jobs a certain amount of time needs to be allocated before the person can be considered fully trained and experienced at the current level of responsibility. It is only after this period of time that it makes sense to begin assessing potential for future advancement.
2. A rating of nonpromotability be recorded before termination be given consideration.

3. A rating of nonpromotability be accompanied by a description of specific reasons for this assessment. These reasons should relate to performance objectives or describe behavioral traits.

Such policy guidelines provide for maximum documentation of the problem areas that led to the negative assessment.

Terminations that conform to the above policy guidelines are not without conflict; lack of conflict is impossible. However, the guidelines can keep conflict to a minimum, increasing the number of instances when things go smoothly. Furthermore, they eliminate emotional terminations on the part of management. Managers are forced into a somewhat reasoned process to support their decisions. Given the traumatic nature of the termination process for both the person being dismissed and the organization, anything less should be singularly unacceptable.

The above guidelines do not unnecessarily hamstring managers in dealing with subordinates. Flexibility can be built into the process. For example, if performance appraisals are given annually, this does not mean that three years are required to discharge a person. Corporate policy can stipulate that when a substandard review is given, the next review can be (or should be) much sooner, perhaps within three months. The point is that managers should be forced to deal with the problem explicitly and in a manner that provides the subordinate ample opportunity to understand his position.

Reasons Unrelated to Performance

Realistically, people are dismissed for reasons other than poor performance. Corporate policy should be oriented toward keeping such instances within specific legitimate limits. Among the reasons for termination that are not related to performance but should be addressed in policy statements are the following:

Reorganization. Often business conditions make it necessary to restructure an organization, and some employees are displaced. In such instances, it should be company policy to initiate a search for alternative employment opportunities within the firm. Only if the search process fails to identify an acceptable position does termination become a feasible alternative. Termination policy should recognize that such circumstances do occur periodically and require that managers substantiate the internal job search process prior to dismissing someone.

Retrenchment. Similar to, and often associated with, reorganization, retrenchment is often necessitated by economic conditions. Again, policy guidelines should reflect the commitment to avoid this alternative whenever possible and require documentation of the specific advantages of the termination to the organization.

In both reorganization and retrenchment, corporate policy should be explicit; bona fide job elimination will have to be documented. Policy should dictate that documentation include how the eliminated job has been replaced or why the task is no longer necessary (for example, duplication of effort needs to be eliminated or a product line has been eliminated).

Consultants see a lot of instances in which a manager talks about job elimination when, in fact, the job has been relocated elsewhere in the department. This usually is an attempt to gloss over a termination as job elimination when the real reason is based on performance. Terminations due to reorganization or retrenchment should be consistent with corporate strategy and not be an isolated decision.

Recognition that reorganization or retrenchment may result in terminations in no way compromises a corporate policy toward job security. Rather, it acknowledges the obvious. We know of a large insurance company whose top officers made repeated speeches and commitments about lifelong job security. The history of this company was, with the exception of severe job negligence, to disavow termination as a matter of corporate policy.

In 1977, severe financial difficulties required a staffing cut of 800 employees. The incongruity was enormous. Recent corporate speeches had guaranteed job security on the one hand while drastic personnel cuts were taking place on the other. Our data indicate that this company's recruiting and managerial credibility will take years to recover.

Recognizing the possibility of termination is not the same as advocating it. In fact, explicit policy in this area can actually serve to reinforce job security. Requiring documentation can make managers more cautious and less spurious in their staffing decisions. The above policy guidelines are clearly intended to make legitimate dismissals possible while simultaneously requiring a thoughtful, reasoned approach. Thus, addressing termination directly can make some executives more deliberative.

Few, if any, corporations can guarantee total job security, especially in the economy of the late twentieth century, with recurring business cycles in the face of persistent inflation. To promise such security is to gamble with corporate credibility. Management can state clearly that maintaining employment is a key corporate objective while acknowledging that under certain last-choice instances, termination may occur.

Ethical Misconduct. This reason has to do with the personal integrity of the employee. Violation of laws is an ethical reason for termination. So too, is any situation in which the individual has misrepresented either himself or some aspect of his work. Such acts must be confronted, since failure to hold the person accountable gives tacit approval to the behavior.

As with all terminations, dismissals on this basis should be well documented. References must be worked out carefully. Unless criminal behavior that the company feels it wants to prosecute is involved, most companies give the person the option of resigning. In any event, unless guilt is legally established, the company might be liable for any accusation that prevents the person from obtaining future employment.

Therefore, when responding to reference checks inquiring why the person left his job, most companies refer to divergence from company policy, failure to comply with procedures, or differences of opinion about management practices. Usually, the company will agree not to go beyond such explanations in exchange for evidence of remorse on the part of the employee who behaved unethically.

Failure to Conform to Conditions of Employment. All organizations maintain policies and procedures designed to control the variation of personal work habits. Policies pertaining to attendance, lateness, break periods, and security are examples. Usually these vary by job classification.

Any employee who regularly fails to comply with such regulations is a candidate for discharge. The key guidelines here are that the standard in question is applied consistently to all employees in a given job classification, that the rule is enforced immediately upon violation, and that the employee has been warned that continued failure to comply would result in termination.

The Refereeing Role of Policy

Earlier we stated that the majority of terminations are traceable to personality clashes; a subordinate does not get along with the boss. This chapter has advocated a set of corporate policy guidelines that place performance or organization-based criteria on the termination process. Do we believe that the above guidelines will really redirect or control the reasons that underlie most terminations? And to what extent can a manager expect to demand a comfortable relationship with a subordinate? The two issues are interrelated.

At the managerial level of an organization, personality often plays a decisive role in determining effectiveness. Indeed, as we have previously noted, stripped to its essentials, the hiring decision boils down to two basic questions: Does the applicant have enough experience and expertise to do the job? Can I work with the person? Once the executive is employed, the elusive difference between effectiveness and ineffectiveness is often personal style—the match between personality and job environment (including the boss's style).

The above policy guidelines do not reverse this reality of organization life so much as referee it. Corporate policy should require that superiors relate issues of style to issues of substance. Essentially, the problem is one of translating personality (for example, overaggressiveness) into specific behavior (failure to consider customer problems) that results in poor performance (loss of sales). Corporate policy can put pressure on managers to make the connection between style and performance. In the absence of this type of connection, questions must be raised about the legitimacy of a termination.

A boss has the right to expect the personal style of a subordinate to contribute to the legitimate goals of the work unit. When a subordinate's personality traits lead him to disregard the directives of his boss, dismissal becomes a reasonable consideration. However, total congruence of personality is not an inherent managerial right. By placing brakes on impulsive termination decisions, policy can force managers into constructive reasoning as to the substance and depth of their complaints about a subordinate.

Complementary to the requirement that the termination be job related is a policy of not terminating for discriminatory reasons—sex, race, religion, or age. Affirmative action programs already reinforce this principle. Termination policy should restate the company position.

The Policy of Managerial Review

Once a decision is made to let someone go, corporate policy should require that it be reviewed at the next level of management before the termination interview takes place. The need for keeping a superior informed on this type of decision might appear obvious, yet, time and time again, outplacement consultants find instances in which a manager became emotional and fired someone on the spot. A policy of managerial review provides for continuity of management. A superior at the next level of management has an opportunity to determine whether the termination is appropriate—indeed, whether or not the problem really lies with the person designated for termination.

For example, in one case we observed, Frank, a manager new to the company, was a bit overzealous in wanting to make good. He began changing policies and procedures almost immediately, often borrowing from what had worked elsewhere for him without appearing to give much thought to his new situation. His aggressiveness caused several employees to resist, and he decided to terminate a couple of them.

Because the two employees had a history of acceptable performance, the manager's superior assessed the situation carefully. He counseled the new manager to soften his approach for a while. With time, the people involved became acclimated to the new situation. Things began to function smoothly and the manager learned something about how to initiate change. In subsequent interviews, one of the employees Frank wanted to dismiss made the following comments: "When Frank first came on board, he was like a bull in a china shop. I think he realized he had to back off a little. A lot of his ideas are good ones. I've learned a lot from him."

The other employee commented: "We had our differences early on. He was trying to do everything like the company he came from. Things have settled down now, though. I think he's more confident, more relaxed. He's done some good things. I think we get along fine, now that we understand each other."

Frank himself remarked: "Early on I misread a few people. I tried to force everything. George [Frank's boss] helped me see that. I took a second look at some of my people; worked with them instead of against them. Some people I had doubts about turned out okay."

The point of this case is not to suggest that if a department is in disarray, the person charged with straightening it out should not be allowed to terminate subordinates. In fact, under exceptional circumstances, a manager can be given the right to terminate without review. However, this should be a specific exception to policy.

Generally, it is good managerial practice to require individual managers to review possible cases of termination with their superior before the termination occurs. As the above instance illustrates, this policy can help avoid hasty and unncessary terminations.

Also, the person in the personnel department responsible for termination policy should be involved *before* a termination occurs. This person can be trained to ensure that the termination is consistent with corporate policy and that the proper support package is prepared, and he can counsel the manager on how to handle the actual termination.

The Support Package

Beyond specifying the grounds for termination, corporate policy should set guidelines as to the nature of the support package given to the terminated executive. The support package is important, since the person will have to rely heavily on it during his search for new employment. Generally, a good support package has the following ingredients:

• Policy should set the parameters of the financial aspects of the support package. Although considerable variation exists in current corporate practices, some general guidelines derived from our experience are:

1. People earning $30,000 and above—two to four months' severance is appropriate.
2. People earning $50,000—five to six months' severance.
3. Above $60,000—a company should consider up to one year of severance.

Although many companies give a lump sum severance payment, we recommend an agreement to allocate monies on a monthly basis, just as if the previous salary and benefits were continuing. We will explore the rationale behind this principle below. Suffice it to say that the company wants to posture itself as paying the person to find a job. Severance payments are best not viewed as some sort of corporate financial booby prize, but as limited assistance for the former employee during the transition period.

• As a matter of policy, benefits and severance compensation should be explained in a letter that the employee can take at the time of termination. This letter, cleared by corporate counsel, should spell out in clear language the nature of financial arrangements. Remember: people are often not thinking clearly during the termination interview. Details of the arrangements are often lost. It is not at all uncommon for a terminated manager to be unaware of the status of his or her financial benefits. Since calling the former boss is awkward, the person often just assumes things, many times to his detriment. The termination letter is a document to which he or she can refer.

• Specific people who can be used as references should be identified. The person should be informed as to what these people are prepared to say regarding the reason for the termination and past performance. In this way, the story the person will tell potential employers can be consistent with what his former employer is saying in references. More importantly, it is clear just whom the individual can use comfortably as a reference, a detail that is often overlooked during terminations.

• Secretarial arrangements for the terminated manager should be made explicit. Practices vary from offering no support, to having a secretary continue to take messages for a specific period of time, to providing complete secretarial support. We recommend that the person have access to a typist who will type his or her résumé and letters as well as take phone messages while that person is seeking employment. At a minimum, this arrangement should exist until the person's severance payments expire.

• The typist can be a member of the company's secretarial staff or of an outside service. In either case, the extent to which the terminated manager can rely on this clerical person for help should be spelled out. Acceptable corporate policy should be decided upon and the guidelines specified. Otherwise, considerable variation in practice is likely to evolve. Variation, among other things, is likely to generate grounds for a discrimination case.

Increasingly, companies are providing job search counseling as part of the severance package. This counseling is provided by either a specialist in the personnel department or an outside counselor, and is intended to soften the blow by giving the terminated person some assistance in organizing a job search. Such counseling can range from specific training in job search skills to career assessment and assistance in helping the person evaluate the events that led to his termination. As the counseling help extends from the limited objective of developing job search skills into other areas of personal support, it takes on the character of true outplacement counseling.

In our experience, such counseling can be one of the most important elements of the support package. Often counseling can prevent the person from making mistakes that squander other aspects of the package. In some cases, it literally helps the person put himself together and provides much needed structure and direction. Later chapters explore this type of counseling in considerable detail.

Making the Policy Decisions

The starting point in developing an effective termination program is to gain corporate agreement on the issues outlined above. The development of a set of policy guidelines should be preceded by a review of past terminations. This analysis of past terminations should look at:

- The grounds for termination, including those based on performance and those based on other factors.
- The documentation of the reasons for termination and whether it was adequate.
- The names and titles of those who reviewed the termination.
- The support package that was provided.

Such an analysis can bring to the surface issues that need to be dealt with both on the policy level and in terms of specific termination practices. Periodic review can help assess compliance with corporate policies once these policies have been put in effect. Compliance reviews can pinpoint areas of weakness in policy or identify steps that need to be taken in support of corporate policy.

Role of the Internal Specialist

If policy is to be converted into practice, a person or persons must be assigned specific responsibility for termination practices. In general, this person will be accountable for maintaining compliance with corporate policy. However, the job contains several more specific functions.

The internal specialist also serves as a point of contact with the corporation for the person who has been discharged. Inevitably, even when there is a specific letter spelling out severance compensation, benefits, and other issues, questions arise. Someone who has been terminated is often confused about whom to contact at the company should he or she have any questions. Typically, the person does not feel comfortable about going back to the boss. As often as not, he or she is even uncomfortable with the personnel department in general. There is a need for someone to be designated as the individual's contact should there be questions about benefits, references, and other such matters.

When the company provides internal outplacement counseling as part of the support package, giving guidance to the terminated person on employment strategy becomes part of the internal specialist's role. If outside consultants are used for this purpose, the internal specialist is the best coordinator for their services.

Counseling managers on how to terminate someone is another aspect of the internal specialist's role. Earlier we recommended that corporate policy require that personnel be notified before the termination interview is conducted. This notice gives the internal specialist the opportunity both to review the documentation and support package material and to discuss how the manager plans to conduct the termination interview. The specialist can lend his expertise on such matters as timing, place, and how to structure the discussion; in short, he or she can sharpen the skills of the manager who will do the firing.

Who Should the Internal Specialist Be?

In large companies of $100 million in sales and up, the nature of the personnel function is changing drastically. Historically, personnel work has been office management and record keeping, with some counseling work included. Today, the traditional functions of personnel are handled by specialized experts. The people side of personnel management is also becoming specialized.

One large New York bank has a Ph.D. psychologist who fills an outplacement counseling role. He does internal outplacement counseling as well as referring people for outside counseling when that best meets their needs. This work is his full-time responsibility.

Another organization has a professional career counselor

who does some outplacement counseling work, but primarily works with people who are disgruntled with their jobs. We could give example after example of similar corporate positions. These types of personnel positions are only starting to emerge. In the future, they will dominate the one-to-one consultation aspects of pesonnel work.

Termination is a difficult experience. The person is confronted not only with sorting out what went wrong in the job, but also with a series of significant decisions about the future. Confused about his or her current status with the company, the individual needs to be able to talk to someone who is trained in counseling skills and knows the situation.

Smaller companies may find that this type of resource on a specialist basis is not always feasible. In these instances, the function may have to be part of a more general personnel manager's job. Nevertheless, such an individual will have to have basic counseling skills in order to do the job effectively. In the future, such skills are likely to be a basic requirement for a personnel manager.

In our experience it is best not to combine the duties of the termination/outplacement specialist and the recruiter. One obvious reason is that the two functions inherently conflict. A company may be recruiting at the same time it is terminating people. To have both groups of people in the same area, waiting to see the same person, creates problems.

One example of these problems came up during a consulting assignment with a major $12 billion organization that had a division undergoing a staff cutback. Almost 400 people were being displaced. The division's recruiting manager was assigned to supervise the outplacement of these people. While one of us was in a meeting with the recruiting manager, a ruckus started in the waiting room. A person was screaming at the receptionist about someone else in the room. When everything calmed down, the recruiting manager explained that this had happened four or five times after a person who was being outplaced learned that temporary help was being hired to cover certain jobs.

Other clients have had similar problems with people being let go encountering people who were being recruited. At best it creates an awkward situation and contributes nothing to making either the recruit or the terminated person comfortable.

Another real dilemma is whether or not recruitment managers have enough time to spend with terminated employees or to monitor termination policy effectively. Terminated employees need time to explain their problems and concerns. Furthermore, managers facing the probability of having to terminate someone require considerable consultation time. Unless the company has a freeze on hiring and no recruiting is taking place, the recruiting manager seldom has time to spend on terminations.

We have observed that people who are geared to recruit are generally different from those who are geared toward counseling and listening to the problems of those being discharged. By and large, the recruiters with whom we have dealt are motivated to go out and find people, sell people on the company, and try to bring in the best possible people. They are not psychologically oriented toward listening to the problems associated with the termination process.

In almost every case we have observed, recruiting managers who have had termination responsibilities for long periods of time have resigned. More than a couple related to us that they were leaving because "dealing with the problems of termination is not my thing." Perhaps the fastest way to lose a recruiting manager is to place him or her in charge of termination policies and practices.

We mention these problems because there seems to be a tendency to combine the recruitment and termination functions. This may be because both functions deal with issues related to the labor market. Often the reasoning is that a recruiter should know where someone can find a job. As we have seen, the two aspects of personnel work are not as closely related as some people think. Of course, in a plant setting, a personnel generalist often has to assume this role along with his other duties.

What are the characteristics of an effective termination specialist? As with many professional positions, there is no one ideal "type" for the emerging job of termination specialist. However, it is possible to describe some potential criteria that should characterize the person filling this role.

The person should be mature and secure. The person selected to do this type of work should exhibit a good understanding of himself and of how he functions in today's changing world. He doesn't have to be an outgoing type of person; it is more important that he feel secure about himself and his skills and abilities.

The termination specialist should be mature in the sense that he has insight into the reasons people fail on the job, and have an understanding of how people who encounter difficulty in one situation often succeed in another. This characteristic is important if the specialist is to have a balanced perspective of the situations he encounters. Actually, his experience must command respect from both management and the people being displaced. Otherwise he will be unable to establish the type of relationship that is necessary to be effective.

The maturity factor is an important one. We find many companies that create the job of internal termination specialist and place young, inexperienced people in this personnel position. These people encounter continual resistance as they attempt to fulfill their role. Often they end up leaving the company. The area of termination is not an easy entry assignment.

The person should be well trained in career guidance counseling. When companies establish the position of internal termination specialist, part of the job assignment virtually always involves outplacement counseling. Thus, the person in the job must have some fundamental counseling skills.

Additionally, the specialist must understand the career assessment process and have the skills necessary to help the terminated person sort out his or her current situation. These skills can be learned and are obtainable from universities as well as career guidance consulting organizations.

We are not talking about a person with a Ph.D.-level training in counseling, but rather someone who has received training in how to avoid creating dependency relationships with dismissed employees. Many displaced employees seek dependency, and are more than willing to let the specialist assume responsibility for them. The primary pitfall confronting the specialist is the tendency to say such things as: "I will help find you a job," or "Don't worry, we will assist you in finding a job quickly." These types of comments make commitments that neither the company nor the counselor can meet. In fact, it is the person's responsibility to find a job; the counselor is there to provide him with skills that can facilitate the job search process.

The person should have a good knowledge of the job market and the job search process. In addition to having basic counseling skills, it is important that the specialist know how the employment process works, especially at the executive level. One of the things a terminated person is looking for is practical advice on what pitfalls to avoid and what steps to take to help facilitate the job search process. Here, again, the mature person has an advantage. He or she can blend outplacement training with experience to provide credible support to the terminated person.

The counselor should be well trained in job search techniques. All too often, corporations today are putting people in the position of specialist to do termination counseling with no career guidance training and only a minimum of training on teaching people how to find another position.

It is interesting to note that most people think they know how to find another job and believe they can counsel someone on how to do so. Most of these people would advise someone to get a résumé together and mail it to search organizations, placement agencies, and corporations. If you think this is the best way to find a job, you are very, very mistaken. However, you hold a majority opinion. There are certain techniques and approaches to finding another position that are mandatory and, if one is going to manage termination counseling or outplacement counseling, one should be well trained in these approaches.

The person should enjoy working with people under duress. The person filling the termination specialist role should have an authentic, constructive feeling for people. So many people say today, "We like to work with people." In reality, most people find this very difficult. The personality makeup of the termination specialist must make him or her secure with other people. This is not a job in which one is going to become a lay psychologist, and the person must be clearly aware that he or she must not meddle in psychological matters. Rather, the termination specialist should be a person who listens well, can give direction and advice, and is sensitive to the trauma that the terminated employee is going through.

People who get into this work often feel sorry for the person who has been terminated. This is a natural human response to someone who is in trouble. Feeling sorry, however, does nothing to help the terminated person and frequently results in the other person becoming depressed himself. Empathy, rather than pity, is required. In other words, it takes a strong person who clearly visualizes himself as helping the terminated employee find a new position, rather than a new life, to be successful at termination counseling.

At Drake Beam Morin, we emphasize that the counselor cannot get too close to the person who has been terminated, if he is, in fact, going to help. Also, understanding the limitations of the counselor's ability to help is the beginning of good job search counseling. The counselor cannot *make* the person successful.

Although many companies look for a Ph.D. in psychology to fill this role, such professional training is not mandatory. Within the framework of the general characteristics previously mentioned, people from a wide range of backgrounds have proved to be effective termination specialists. Those with corporate experience, rounded out with a personnel management background and basic counseling training, are capable of performing very effectively.

Management Training in Support of Policy

Corporate policies are limited in their impact if managers are not trained to implement them. In the area of termination, this training is of two kinds. The first is of an informational nature. Managers must be knowledgeable about corporate policy and understand the mechanics of applying it. For example, all managers must be aware that a poorly completed performance appraisal can prevent or delay an attempt to terminate someone. Also, managers must have a working knowledge of what constitutes a legitimate reason for termination.

The second type of training is in skill development. Managers must be capable of conducting a reasonably effective termination interview. Knowing how to organize the discussion and having the capability to retain control of the meeting are issues of managerial skill. Being able to open the interview properly, handle defensiveness, and close the discussion are equal matters of skill. Chapter 6 identifies these skills in some detail.

Many of these skills are basic to the managerial process, including such activities as selection interviewing, job coaching, and performance appraisal. Others are specific to the termination process. Time should be allocated for training managers in how to use these skills in corporate managerial skill development programs. These skills can be reinforced by the internal specialist when termination occurs.

After the Employee Is Gone

Our discussion in this chapter has focused on issues that either lead up to or support the termination. Once the employee leaves, however, the company still has problems with which to conern itself. Two in particular are references and the co-workers of the terminated person.

References

With the Freedom of Information Act, reference giving has become more sensitive, since applicants may ask to see submitted references. A reference that unfairly damages the terminated employee's job search can land the company in court.

Therefore, it is important that company references be submitted only by people who have been previously identified to the terminated person. The content of the references should not deviate from what was discussed at the time of termination. All inquiries about the terminated person should be referred to either these people or the specialist in the personnel department. In fact, as a matter of policy, reference inquiries about employees who have left the firm should be referred to the personnel department unless the manager receiving the inquiry has previously agreed to provide a reference.

By law, all that is required is that former employers confirm the fact that the person in question did work at the company for a specified period of time. Any other information is not required and may, in fact, harm the organization that released the employee. However, it is good practice to agree on the answers to two questions at the time of discharge: What kind of employee (or manager) was the person? What happened to cause the person to leave? Refusing to address these issues in references can place the person in a prejudicial light and can hamper his job search.

What Kind of Employee Was the Person? When answering the question of what kind of employee or manager the person was, it is best to keep statements positive. This does not mean the reference should be unnecessarily rosy or misleading in any way. Rather, strengths, not weaknesses, should be highlighted. The kind of environment in which the person is likely to perform well rather than situations in which the person is not likely to do well should be described.

For example, if a person has had difficulty in getting organized, you do not have to say that he has poor organizational skills. Rather, the reference should describe either a strength or a situation that won't expose the person's weakness. Perhaps it could say that this person works best in spontaneous and unstructured environments.

Why Was He or She Let Go? This question is more difficult to answer. In sensitive instances, we recommend a statement to the effect that "we agreed to disagree." Use of words such as "we let him go" or "we terminated the relationship" generate a range of negative images in the minds of prospective employers. A company should stay away from these kinds of statements and instead make reference to a situation in which the employer and employee agreed that a change was advisable. It is best to avoid the issue of why the person left unless it is explicitly asked or the reason does not reflect on the person's behavior (for example, a staff reduction).

On the following page is a sample recommendation letter. Notice that it verifies length of employment and scope of responsibility. The letter also highlights the person's special strengths—his ability to improve organization and control on an operation, and his technical knowledge.

Although it mentions that Harvey left the company, the reference avoids placing fault or blame. Rather, it states only that Harvey and his boss disagreed. How that disagreement is assessed by the new employer is left for discussions between Harvey and him. The letter concludes with a comment that indicates the writer remains appreciative of Harvey's abilities and past contributions, which is true.

Harvey had been dismissed because he never really accepted a reorganization of the company, and was continually battling over old issues. His failure to cooperate completely with associates was undermining his effectiveness as a manager, as key decisions got bogged down in discussions of organization.

Mr. Jerome Brown
XL Corporation
New York, New York

Dear Mr. Brown:

   I am writing at the request of Harvey Wilson in
support of his candidacy for the position of director of
manufacturing with your firm. I am pleased to learn of
the possibility that Harvey might be associated with
your organization.

   Harvey was with us for nine years, during which time
he was promoted twice. He worked under me for five
years as general manager of production. Harvey's particular strengths include an ability to organize and
control a rapidly growing operation. He personally
developed and implemented many of the operations procedures that allowed us to retain control of our diverse
production operations. His knowledge of process technology is second to none and he earned the respect of his
subordinates. At the time he left us, Harvey was responsible for nine plant locations, all of which employed
between 500 and 1,000 people.

   As you know, Harvey left us three months ago. There
were several changes occurring in our business and we
agreed to disagree. It was a difficult time for all of
us, but he left with my respect for his abilities and
accomplishments.

   From what he has told me, I am confident he can make
a contribution to your company.

                          Best wishes,

                          John Simpson
                          Vice President

If the reasons for the dismissal are so severe that the company cannot be comfortable following the above guidelines, the agreement with the employee should be that the company will only provide verification of employment.

We cannot recommend too strongly that the whole subject of references be thoroughly discussed with the employee before he or she leaves the premises. Our counselors find that for over 40 percent of the people who have extended difficulty in finding new employment the problem can be traced to a poor reference.

Dealing with Employees Who Remain

Dealing with the employees who remain is an important issue. When a person or group of people is severed from an organization, one of the most overlooked items on management's list of things to do is what to say to the employees left behind. It seems that when a person is terminated, management gives a sigh of relief the day the termination is over and is not aware of the hard feelings and mistrust that remain with the employees who stay on with the company.

When someone is dismissed for cause, the manager doing the termination should inform other employees in the work unit that "John will be leaving the company effective as of June 2, and we wish him the best in future endeavors." This can be done verbally or by memo. A manager should neither encourage nor discourage inquiries about the termination. If he feels certain people are upset, the manager can privately ask whether John's leaving has bothered them. Otherwise, the initiative can be left to the employees.

When he gets into a discussion about the dismissal, the boss should be willing to talk, but stress that he cannot, with integrity, share information of a personal nature. Obvious job failures can be pointed out. Management should also stress that the problems had been the topic of frequent discussions between the manager and the dismissed employee. It should be noted that the employee was aware that if certain changes did not take place, termination would occur. Depending on the agreement that has been reached with the dismissed employee, management's response to inquiries from other employees should reflect the position that "we mutually agreed John was ready for a change."

Management comments should be honest; there is no need to lie about the situation. On the other hand, the details of the termination should remain the personal business of the employee. Most people recognize a person's right to privacy and will respect management for guarding it. If it is clear that the severance was on unfriendly terms, the manager should respond to any verbal inquiries by commenting that significant disagreement existed, and we made what we feel is the right decision for both parties.

The concern most employees have is whether the person was treated fairly, and, especially, whether he knew that his performance was unacceptable. This reflects on their own concern about job security. Essentially, management's position should be:

- Any decision about the person's future was not made abruptly but, rather, was the culmination of many discussions with the individual.
- Management felt the change was necessary.
- Not all the facts are known to others, and management does not feel it appropriate to go into detail.
- The manager is willing to discuss with any employee his or her own job situation.

Occasionally, a dismissed employee will complain to his peers about how badly he was treated. If confronted with such complaints, management should point out that a significant difference of opinion existed and that there were factors other than those the person is citing.

A manager should emphasize that what is important is not what happened to the dismissed employee, but other employees' job performance. In discussions with other employees, the manager should ask whether they are comfortable in their own positions, if they are unsure about where they stand, or if they have been unfairly treated. If the answer is no, the manager should indicate that this is because their performance is satisfactory and they have good communication with him. If the employees hesitate or give a yes answer, the manager should attempt to identify what can be done to improve the situation.

The principle is straightforward. Impress upon subordinates that the manager has, and wants to maintain, an effective working relationship with them. That is the appropriate concern. Comparison with the other person is not relevant or appropriate other than to stress that the termination was not a surprise to the person involved.

If more than one person has been terminated, such as in a cutback situation, the first step is to tell the remaining employees that the severances are over. To the best of management's ability, it should explain the reasons for the cutback thoroughly. If there is a strong possibility of future cutbacks, that, too, should be noted. The key to maintaining credibility is honesty.

We know of one organization that finds it difficult to obtain or maintain new talent because of the way in which it dealt with a series of group severances between 1967 and 1969. More than ten years later, the company has to pay extra to recruit good people because of its reputation. Recruiters are often told by potential employees that they are not interested because "the word is you can't be sure of where you stand."

Interestingly enough, even when employees know there is a possibility of future cutbacks, most stay on. Lack of management credibility can hurt an organization more than a frank presentation of even bleak organization prospects.

Once the terminations are concluded, managers should initiate discussions with remaining employees about future prospects, including how they might affect their careers. The concern most people will have is over job security and future prospects at the company. These issues should be addressed directly and not left to the rumor mill.

Criteria for a Successful Termination

The methods described above are the key to terminating someone in a manner that minimizes the cost to both the company and the person involved. The following checklist summarizes points made in this chapter. As such, it constitutes a working set of criteria for successful terminations.

- Sufficient grounds for termination
  Not trumped up
  Well documented
- Well-written and effectively communicated appraisals pre-ceding the termination (if performance based)
  Three or more
  Acknowledged by the employee
- Termination review
  By next level of management
  By the personnel department
- Terminating manager trained in termination procedures
  Understands company policy
  Understands how to structure the termination interview
  Has skills required to conduct the interview
- Sufficient support package
  Severance payments in line with company policy
  Reliable references identified and agreed upon
  Secretarial support
  Benefits written out in severance letter
  Predetermined contact for communication with the com-pany
  Counseling available on how to find employment
- Follow-up
  References are consistent
  Employees notified that the person is leaving

4

Dealing with a Nonexempt Employee

T HE FOCUS OF RECENT LITERATURE ON OUT-placement has been directed toward managerial or administrative employees. Yet a large number of the people fired every year by large corporations do not fall into that category. Nonexempt workers—white collar and blue collar—inevitably suffer the most when a company has cutbacks and, in the absence of a collective bargaining agreement, are most likely to be terminated for disciplinary or performance reasons.

With two notable exceptions, the worker is without legal protection from dismissal. As noted earlier, common law has pretty much upheld the employer's right to dismiss employees, regardless of the fairness or justice of the cause. The exceptions are those employees who are protected by collective bargaining agreements or members of the protected classes under EEO legislation.

Collective bargaining agreements customarily protect employees from being dismissed without just cause. Furthermore, such contracts provide remedies for redress when an employee feels his or her termination has been unjust. Disputes are regularly arbitrated under the guidelines of collective agreements.

Civil rights legisiation outlaws dismissal for reasons of age, race, nationality, religion, or sex. An employee who feels his discharge was discriminatory in nature can attempt redress through these statutes. The effort is easier if the person being fired is over 40, a member of a racial minority, or a woman. A broad range of people, however, have tried to stretch civil rights laws to categorize their dismissals as discriminatory, usually because, not being covered by a union contract, they have no other avenue of legal recourse.

Traditional Nonconcern

Not only has the law provided little or no protection, but companies have seldom been concerned about assisting nonexempts who are being terminated. Generally, the corporate attitude has been that these employees can go next door and find a job. Since they were never part of the management team, the sense of corporate obligation is typically less than when an administrative employee is concerned.

As is so often the case, reality is somewhat different. Finding another job is frequently not as simple as going down the street. Average periods of unemployment range from three months to one year, depending on the economy and the transfer ability of one's skills. Secretarial and certain mechanical skills are more easily exported to other companies than those of other nonexempts who, in effect, have skills only within the context of their former jobs. Assemblers are an example. In the general labor market, assemblers are semiskilled or unskilled workers. Typically the only organization that has a need for a "Class II" assembler is the company that has just dismissed the person or a direct competitor.

Often nonexempts have limited financial resources and are not as geographically mobile as managerial workers. Yet they are the least likely to be provided with any support package. The degree of psychological trauma connected with being terminated is, by and large, the same for a nonexempt employee as it is for an exempt one. We have worked with people who have been in the secretarial ranks for 10 or 15 years and thought the company would take care of them until retirement. These people are often in shock when their jobs are part of a general cutback or they are terminated for whatever reason. Most of these people do not understand how this could happen to them, and they sometimes find themselves in what we call the "brittle case" category. In essence, a brittle case is someone who cannot go out and find another job because of the degree of trauma connected with the termination. The shock is such that he or she feels as if another job will never be available.

Although not every nonexempt has such a severe reaction, being dismissed generates the same problems that it does for the exempt employee. Learning how to apply for a job, whom to use for a reference, how to explain what happened on the last job, and how to deal with family and peer pressure and one's own reactions of failure and frustration are dilemmas everyone faces, not just managerial personnel.

Termination Policy for the Nonexempt Employee

As with all employees, the foundation for termination policy at this level of the organization should be just cause. The concept of just cause is given teeth by requiring supervisors to provide documentation of repeated failure of the subordinate to meet performance standards or comply with company regulations or to provide substantive business reasons for eliminating a position.

When a worker is abusing company standards, failure to apply discipline undermines the supervisor's ability to maintain control over the work unit. Behavioral scientists recognize "equity" as a strong need that motivates worker behavior. Advanced by J. Stacy Adams, equity theory maintains that workers continually compare the quality of their inputs and the level of their outcomes against those of their co-workers.[1] Inputs are characteristics the worker brings to or inserts in the job (skills, education level, experience, motivational effort, and so on). Outcomes are the benefits derived from the job (compensation, status, and so on).

Equity theory holds that when workers perceive an unfavorable ratio of their own inputs and outcomes to those of others, a psychological tension is created. The worker strives to release this tension by reducing or increasing either his inputs or his outcomes. For example, an employee who perceives his job qualifications as being greater than those of co-workers receiving the same pay might produce less work in order to reduce the inequity.

Equity theory has special relevance in the disciplinary process. When one worker violates work rules, such as being repeatedly late for work, a state of inequity is created. Other workers view their inputs (showing up on time) as being greater than the tardy person's. Most of them look for the supervisor to restore equity to the work situation by imposing discipline. Every consultant has heard complaints during interviews about a supervisor who lets people "get away with murder."

If the supervisor fails to restore equity through the use of disciplinary methods, eventually employees will move to restore equity to the situation by reducing their own inputs; they, too, fail to comply with the regulation. Soon the supervisor finds even his good employees violating the rule. Discipline is a tool for maintaining equity in the work situation. Failure to use it as such leads to wider control problems as employees take the initiative in restoring equity.

When the employee's behavior is the cause for termination, documentation of at least three warning discussions should be

[1]J. Stacy Adams, "Toward an Understanding of Inequity, *Journal of Abnormal Psychology* (Vol. 67, 1963a).

required. When terminating any employee, the supervisor should be required to demonstrate that the worker was aware that his current behavior was not acceptable, was informed as to what was expected in the future, and repeatedly failed to meet that standard.

Over the years, the arbitration of labor disputes has resulted in general guidelines of industrial relations in the area of discipline and dismissal. The principles that guide the arbitration process are instructive for any corporate policy aimed at establishing fair employee relations practices. Some of the more significant ones are cited below.

Termination should not be used as a punitive tool. Obviously, dismissing someone from his job is one of the harsher disciplinary sanctions available to supervisors. In that sense, it is punitive in nature. Termination, however, should be the end result of a series of disciplinary measures, and it should never be used to "get someone" or to make an example of someone. It is in that sense that we use the term "nonpunitive."

If a work standard has not been enforced in the past, it is incumbent on the part of the supervisor to warn all employees that in the future the rule will be enforced. By not enforcing the rule, supervisors have given tacit approval of employee behavior on the job. Thus, employees have every right to expect that the rule will be overlooked in the future. Employees must be put on notice that supervisors are changing their attitude toward enforcement. Otherwise discipline, including termination, is excessively punitive in nature.

Of equal importance is ensuring that disciplinary proceedings are applied to all employees. Failure to perform to organization standards should invoke the same penalty, regardless of the person involved. When failure to invoke disciplinary sanctions becomes a form of reward for an otherwise good employee, the disciplinary process is undermined and again takes on an excessively punitive connotation. Because termination is the end result of the disciplinary process, or the harshest form of discipline, any failure to apply sound disciplinary practice undercuts corporate termination policy.

Termination should be part of a progressive process of applying sanctions. As implied above, termination should be management's last recourse when other disciplinary efforts have failed. Only the harshest employee behavior should meet with immediate dismissal. Other actions should invoke a progressive process in which the supervisor first counsels the employee, then gives a series of warnings and perhaps even time off the job before finally terminating the person. Even when the supervisor feels there is little hope that the person will change, it is important to go through the entire process, giving the person ample and fair opportunity to improve.

The employee should always know the consequences of failing to respond to the current disciplinary measures. When an employee is discharged and can effectively argue that he or she was unaware of the consequences of failing to respond to previous measures that resulted in dismissal, arbitrators have not upheld the dismissal. Their decisions are based on sound industrial relations practice. From the standpoint of fairness and making sure that the lines of communication are not confused, whenever an employee is given a warning or is counseled, the supervisor should inform the person of the next step in the disciplinary process, especially if it involves a substantial penalty.

Supervisors should inform the subordinate of the next step in the disciplinary process even when it can be reasonably argued that the employee should know what that step is. For example, most large corporations publish the steps of the disciplinary process in their employee handbooks. New employees are informed of these steps at the time of employment.

Under such conditions, supervisors often feel that employees know exactly where they stand; as indeed they often do. Still, informing the person of the next disciplinary step, especially if it involves time off or discharge, is the best practice for guaranteeing that the worker is aware of the consequences of his actions. Failure to do so undermines the concept of fair warning.

When applying discipline the supervisor should establish with the employee what can be done in order to get out from under the disciplinary process. As we have stated repeatedly throughout the book, when working with an employee whose performance is getting him into difficulty, the supervisor should state clearly what the expectations are with regard to improvement. At the end of every disciplinary session, not only should the employee be aware of the consequences of failing to improve, but there should be a statement regarding what the employee can do not only to avoid further disciplinary action but also, in effect, to get back in good standing with the supervisor.

Although many times the supervisor may feel that such a change is unlikely, it is always worth the effort to give the individual an opportunity to improve and, if performance does come up to standard, to try to put the current problems in the past.

Documentation of each of the above principles should exist before the termination is initiated. Once the supervisor begins the disciplinary process, it is important that documentation be compiled. The purpose of documentation is not to threaten the employee as much as to communicate the seriousness of the situation and provide a record of what has transpired. Often the documentation itself convinces the employee that the time has come to improve, avoiding the necessity of termination.

At every disciplinary interview the supervisor should note the time, place of discussion, problem discussed, employee reaction, and next step to be taken. It is important that the supervisor note what the next disciplinary step will be, along with the required standard for improvement. It should be noted that failure to meet that standard will be cause for further disciplinary action.

The employee should be asked to sign and date the document. If the employee refuses, the document should be witnessed by another representative of management after being reviewed with the employee present. In either case, the supervisor should also sign and date the document. A minimum of three such documents should precede dismissal. The third of these written warnings often involves a suspension period.

When a decision is made to terminate a nonexempt, it should be reviewed by the next level of management and by the personnel manager before any action is taken. This review should concern itself with determining that the above principles have been followed. Here is a checklist that can be used in the review process. Following this checklist virtually guarantees that a termination is fair and can be substantiated.

1. Documentation of just cause:
    Repeated failure to meet performance standards
    Lack of compliance with company regulations
    Job elimination part of corporate cutbacks
2. If disciplinary in nature:
    Is the termination the final step of a progressive process of applying sanctions?
    Has the employee been informed that the termination is the next step if improvement is not made?
    Does the employee know what level of performance is expected to avoid termination?
    Has each of the above been documented (at least three signed and dated letters)?
3. Managerial review:
    Department management
    Personnel department
4. Severance package:
    Payments
    Contact for recommendations identified and agreed to
    Counseling by personnel arranged
5. Termination interview:
    In private
    Direct, with statement of cause

The Support Package for Nonexempts

A clean termination of a nonexempt employee requires a support package (just as in the case of exempts). The person should get severance pay consistent with tenure and skill level with the company. This may range from a week to a couple of months compensation. It is also good practice to provide a letter specifying whom the employee can use as a reference and what will be said in the reference. This can be given to the employee by the supervisor doing the termination. This information should also be communicated verbally during the termination interview.

A nonexempt employee is just as likely to be in a state of confusion over being terminated as an exempt one. He or she is also as likely to benefit from advice on the job search process. Therefore, counseling arranged through the personnel department is a highly appropriate part of the support package.

Today, more and more companies are providing counseling assistance to severed nonexempt employees. This assistance ranges from providing a workbook on "how to find another job" to offering outplacement counseling with a reputable firm. Between these extremes are various half- to full-day seminars conducted by personnel specialists in either a group or individual setting.

Although such counseling efforts are generally not as elaborate as the support offered exempts, personnel experts are coming to agree on certain topics that are important to nonexempts:

- How to fill out application forms
- How to be interviewed
- How to identify jobs to which their skills are transferable
- Income tax exemptions of job search expenses
- How to determine "what I want to do with the rest of my life."

Nonexempts also need to let off steam and to sort through what has happened. Often this need is as strong as the need for job search skills, although it is less likely to be provided.

We suggest that a representative of the personnel department be available to meet with the employee after the dismissal by the supervisor. This person can review the events that led to the discharge, provide some hints on what to do next, and generally spend time helping the person calm down and collect his or her thoughts. If possible, job search counseling should be provided the following day. Such training is more likely to be beneficial once the employee has overcome the initial shock of the termination. The terminated employee is also more likely to ask questions after having a day to think through the situation.

Rationalizations aside, the reason nonexempts have been excluded from such counseling support has more to do with their status in the workplace than with their actual needs. Management simply has not viewed them as worthy of such support. Extending such considerations to nonexempts meets very real individual and corporate needs. At the same time, it helps break down the class distinctions that exist in the workplace, which tend to reinforce an adversary posture between nonexempts and administrative and managerial employees. Increasingly, programs breaking down these barriers are becoming part of the foundation of enlightened human resource administration.

The Termination Interview

The termination interview should be direct and to the point. Once the employee is seated in the supervisor's office—the termination should be done in private, not in front of other workers—the supervisor should simply begin by stating: "John, I am very sorry, but we are going to have to let you go. You missed your shift three times again this month [or whatever the reason for termination]." The supervisor should refer to the previous disciplinary interviews, stating that the employee was told that failure to improve would result in termination.

Next, the supervisor should inform the employee of his

severance package. The supervisor should not argue with the employee but make it clear that the decision is final. Above all, he should not make any promises to the employee. The employee should be sent to the personnel department for final counseling and to make any grievances.

It is best for the employee to collect his or her things, go to the personnel department for counseling, and then leave the premises. The person needs support and time to assimilate what has happened. Returning to the work unit does little good and can do damage if the employee is working around equipment in a distracted state.

As with exempt employees, the timing should not be at the end of the week or the end of the day. All too often nonexempt terminations occur at 5:00 P.M. on Friday for "payroll purposes," leaving the employee to go home in a state of shock.

After the Employee Leaves

Virtually all labor agreements provide for an appeal process that affords the employee an opportunity to dispute his dismissal. A final step in this process is the opportunity of having his case reviewed by an independent arbitrator. In nonunion companies the sole and final source of appeal is the personnel director. Only a couple of nonunion companies provide for outside arbitration as part of their personnel policy. However, we strongly support this unique practice.

When other nonexempts view a colleague's dismissal, it is easy for them to conclude that the company was arbitrary in its judgment. If the supervisor's case is legitimate, well documented, and in compliance with corporate policy, management has little to fear from arbitration proceedings. The more substantial the case, the less likely the employee is to appeal it. Furthermore, a decision in favor of management removes doubts from the minds of other employees about management's fairness. Finally, the availability of arbitration reinforces company policy. It demonstrates management's confidence in its termination policy and places pressure on supervisors to follow policy practices carefully.

Having such a policy provides an atmosphere of security for employees regarding their rights on the job. It can be a vehicle for contributing to a climate of support and trust between management and nonexempt employees. Above all, it is a practical demonstration that employees don't need a union to protect them from unjust dismissal.

Management is becoming increasingly sophisticated in battling the efforts of unionization. Indeed, proponents of the "quality of work life" movement in industry argue that productivity gains are possible, while maintaining a nonunion environment, if management recognizes the need for workers to have an element of discretion over their jobs and protection from arbitrary management practices. Fair and consistent discharge practices are an important element in the establishment of a positive quality-of-work-life climate. Establishing arbitration rights for employees can greatly reinforce such practices, while providing workers with a tangible source of protection against unfair dismissal.

The practices recommended above are clearly consistent with our previous discussions of appropriate corporate policy. When dealing with nonexempts, although the extent of the benefits may not be the same as for managerial employees, the basic principles and practices should remain the same.

Part II

MANAGING THE TERMINATION PROCESS

If termination policies and procedures are to be effective, managers must be capable of implementing them. In the final analysis, the quality of the interpersonal process between manager and subordinate determines the impact of policy on the person being terminated. Part II deals with the termination process itself. Chapter 5 addresses the corrective coaching process that should precede the termination decision. In Chapter 6, a model for conducting the actual termination interview is provided.

Chapter 7 addresses the outplacement process that many corporations are making available after the termination occurs. In Chapter 8 this process is examined from the counseling perspective.

Chapter 9 looks at six termination situations that often cause problems for managers.

5

Coaching the Ineffective Employee

ALTHOUGH TERMINATION IS OFTEN NECESsary, under most circumstances a manager's first responsibility is to attempt to improve the subordinate's performance. Efforts at coaching his or her performance should occur when there is some skepticism as to the person's ability to improve. Consider, for example, the case of John Strauss.

John Strauss was director of a division that provided professional services to other companies. Although the market for the type of services John's division provided was growing, the size of John's group had remained stagnant for several years. Also, his division had not expanded the range of services it offered clients, and several high-potential, young staff members had left the organization.

As part of the corporate growth strategy, the parent corporation purchased an independent firm that was a competitor of John's group. As part of the merger agreement, the president of the purchased firm was to become the senior manager over John's division, and both staffs were to be integrated into one unit. John was to remain in place, although in a subordinate position to the person coming in from the outside.

Fred Eliot, the person who was brought in over John, was charged by senior management with establishing a growth pattern in the division comparable to that experienced by his firm when it had been an independent operation. Both Fred and corporate management viewed John Strauss as a weak and ineffective manager.

At the time he took over the division, Fred believed it was unrealistic to expect significant improvement in John's performance. John was set in his ways and comfortable in his slot and, despite obvious anxiety over having been placed in a subordinate position to Fred, he did not appear about to change his behavior to any great degree.

In deference to John's seniority with the firm, Fred decided it was reasonable to attempt to identify projects that both were meaningful for the growth of the division and would provide John with an opportunity to demonstrate that he was capable of making a valuable contribution to the company. These special assignments would have the added benefit of not reducing John's work to the same level as that of his immediate subordinates. On the other hand, Fred resolved that if John did not perform well on these assignments, other arrangements, including the possibility of discharge, would have to be made.

Fred gave considerable thought to which projects would be especially suited to John's talents. He wanted to assign work that would be challenging and important but not impossible. Once he had decided on the specific tasks he wanted John to undertake, he arranged a meeting and the two sat down and reviewed John's job assignments for the coming year.

Fred was very specific about what was expected. Each job assignment stated exactly what was to be accomplished, the extent of the work to be done, and the date by which Fred expected John to have completed the work. John complained that some of these projects were not the type of thing that he had done in the past, and that they were not part of his job. Fred, however, made it clear that John's job assignment was important to the division and reflected his professional experience. He also made it clear that these were the kinds of responsibilities he needed John to assume. Prior to sitting down with John, Fred had already reviewed the assignments he intended to give John with the boss, and he was confident of support from higher management.

Thus, when John complained about certain aspects of the work, Fred listened to him, asked him precisely what his concerns were, attempted to identify realistically what kinds of support John would need to get the work done, but made it absolutely clear that he expected John to meet the specified level of performance. Fred also indicated that he planned to sit down with John in five weeks to review the progress that had been made on his assignments.

Five weeks later Fred sat down with John for a progress review. As it turned out, John had not made much headway on any of his assignments. Several of them had not been started at all, while an inadequate effort had been made on others. Fred informed John that his progress was unacceptable and began exploring why more headway had not been made. At the end of the discussion, Fred again told John that it was important that he meet his job objectives and indicated that in about four weeks they would again meet to discuss progress.

Four weeks later, it became clear that John had still not made much progress. Fred once again listened to John's reasons for a lack of progress and also specified interim objectives he wanted to see achieved in each of the areas on which John was working. These interim objectives were set for three weeks.

When John failed to meet most of his interim objectives, Fred told him that he was unhappy with his performance to date and that significant improvement would have to be forthcoming in the future. He also reviewed the notes from each of their meetings, commenting that John was compiling a very unimpressive performance record. Continuation of such poor performance would result in termination.

He also called John's attention to the many changes that

were being made in the division, the new services that were being added, and the opportunities for existing staff to take on increased responsibility for growth and advancement of the division. Fred indicated to John that it was his hope that he would be able to make an important contribution to these changes and that the projects he had been assigned were very relevant to what was happening.

Fred expressed hope that John would recognize that he was being given an opportunity to become an important part of the division and, perhaps in the future, to hold a position of higher responsibility. At the conclusion of the meeting, interim objectives with regard to how much progress was expected within the next three weeks were specified.

At the end of the three weeks, John again fell short on his objectives. This time Fred told John that problems were being created by his lack of progress. Consequently, Fred was going to assign some of the projects to other staff members. Once more Fred reiterated his hope that John would improve his performance and again he set specific interim objectives for the activities that remained.

At this point, it had become clear that John was not making any effort to improve his performance. When he once again failed to meet his interim objectives, Fred indicated that he was going to talk the matter over with senior management and then make a decision as to what should be done at this point in time. He again told John that his failure to make progress on his objectives was moving him closer to being discharged.

In discussions with management, the decision was made to give John a last chance by assigning him to a special project that needed to be done—one that required significant professional experience.

Fred sat down with John and explained that although no progress had been made on previous job objectives, he was being given a special assignment of importance to the organization.

Fred told John that management viewed this as his last chance to prove he could really perform in the new climate of growth that was being established within the organization. Failure to perform would mean dismissal. Again, Fred set interim target dates so that John would have a timetable with which to gauge his progress in completing the project. The project was one that should have taken close to four months to complete. Fred indicated that he would be sitting down with John within two weeks to monitor how much headway had been made.

Again John failed to make any significant progress on his new objective. In fact, after two and a half months, Fred informed senior management that if the project were to be completed he would have to assign somebody else to work on it. Management decided to allow John the full four months to complete the project in order to have given him the entire time allotted. As you might surmise, at the end of four months, John had not come close to completing the project and it was assigned to someone else.

At this time, Fred initiated termination proceedings against John and he was discharged from the organization.

A Point of Comparison

John's performance was in marked contrast to that of Susan Newburg. Susan was a member of John's staff and, like many of the people who worked under John, had not really given evidence of superior motivation or ability. In fact, when Fred came in, he was uncertain as to what real potential existed within the division. He suspected that many of the high-potential people had already left. He resolved, however, to go through a similar process with all members of the staff.

As he had with John, Fred sat down with Susan and outlined specific performance targets and assignments he wanted completed. Once again, each of these assignments was written in terms of the specific end result expected and a timetable was set for completion. In many respects, the activities Fred assigned Susan represented a departure from the type of assignments she had been given in the past.

When Fred sat down for a progress review with Susan, however, it was evident that a lot of headway had been made. In fact, Susan had invested a significant amount of energy in her assignments and was ahead of the specified timetable. The longer Fred worked with Susan, the more it became evident that the activities assigned to her were not ambitious enough. Her positive attitude caused her to be given increased responsibilities. Within a year and a half, she was promoted to a new job that had opened up within the division. Susan's outstanding performance was representative of the kind of improvement noted in many members of the staff.

Analysis of the Case

Unfortunately, Fred's work with John did not have a happy ending; John was eventually terminated. However, the process Fred went through with John was extremely effective and represented a professional approach to the problem. The key element that charcterized Fred's approach was a continuing effort to establish clarity with John.

Clarity is one of the important parts of the job-coaching process. It is vitally important that the person being coached have a clear understanding of exactly what the boss's expectations are and that the boss consider these expectations to be fair and consistent with what is expected of others within the organization. Fred was very careful to establish specific objectives with John and specified exactly what the end results of his efforts should be, the extent to which these end results were to be achieved, and when they should be achieved. These objectives then became the controlling factor Fred used in discussing John's current performance.

The clarity that came out of this process helped guarantee

that every effort was made to ensure that John was getting the message about how Fred viewed his performance. As the process continued, Fred was careful to make sure that John understood the downsides of not performing. Early on, when no progress was evident, he began emphasizing to John that thorough documentation was being made of his performance and that, if progress was not forthcoming, this documentation would provide the basis for discussions with management about his future.

Fred made it clear to John that his retention with the organization was contingent upon his performance against these objectives. By the same token, Fred also took pains to emphasize to John the opportunities opening up within the division and told him that if he did perform, he had a real opportunity to redeem his reputation and become a candidate for advancement. In other words, it was made clear to John at every point in the process that there was a downside risk of not performing as well as an upside opportunity that could be realized if he improved his performance.

It was hoped that John would take advantage of the opportunity and would make a sincere effort at trying to improve his performance. Unhappily, this was not the case. However, because Fred took such a thorough approach to the coaching process, when the distasteful decision to let John go was being considered, it was clear that it was the correct decision for the organization to make.

John had been given every opportunity to perform and had chosen not to respond. Not only that, there was written documentation that John was aware of the stakes involved in terms of his eventual termination. Therefore, although Fred found it distasteful to inform John that he was being let go, he had ample evidence of nonperformance to handle the interview comfortably and in a professional fashion.

The same process revealed untapped potential in the case of Susan Newburg. Here the ending was much happier and resulted in her turning into a strong performer.

The Coaching Process

The coaching process should be characterized by two critical parts: setting specific objectives and holding frequent progress reviews.

Setting Specific Objectives

When specific objectives are set, the subordinate knows exactly what is expected of him. Furthermore, the manager has a benchmark to which he can keep referring in future discussions about the subordinate's performance.

As we have repeatedly stressed, the existence of specific goals is an important part of the conditions that should exist prior to termination. The confusion or uncertainty that often characterizes the reaction of subordinates when they are told they are terminated is created by the absence of specific objectives against which they were expected to perform.

The objectives should be characterized by three elements:

1. They should be oriented toward end results.
2. They should specify the exact extent of achievement the manager expects.
3. They should be tied to a timetable.

When we talk about orienting the objectives to end results, we mean that the goals should specify what should be observably different as a result of the subordinate's performance on the job. All too often, employees expect to be evaluated on the basis of how much effort they are putting into the job rather than what they are accomplishing. This is especially true of people who are weak performers. It is absolutely critical that the manager make it clear that certain outcomes are expected and that the subordinate is being held accountable for these outcomes.

Failure to write objectives that are oriented to end results will do nothing more than get the manager involved in a series of arguments with the subordinate about how the job is going and will not make things much easier if eventually the subordinate has to be dismissed.

Today, many organizations have some form of MBO process as part of their business planning or performance appraisal efforts. In the absence of a formal MBO system, however, the manager can still sit down and specify the exact criteria against which he expects the subordinate to perform.

In addition to specifying the end result, it is important that the manager be specific as to the extent to which the end result should be achieved. For example, it is one thing to say that a subordinate is being held accountable for an increase in business volume in his or her particular region. It is another thing to specify that the individual should achieve at least a 6 percent increase in business volume. By specifying the 6 percent, the manager clarifies still further what is expected of the subordinate's performance.

As much as possible, the end result should be expressed in quantitative terms—percentage of increase, real-dollar volume increase, percentage of critical incidents, or any measure of this nature against which someone's performance can be judged.

In the absence of quantitative measures, objectives should be written in such a way that it is clear that the person either has achieved the objective or has not. For example, in a staff function where the individual is being held accountable for preparing certain reports or certain studies for use in the corporation, the objectives should specify not only that the projects or reports are to be completed, but that they be accepted and used by certain critical managers within the organization. Thus, it is not just the completion of the report but acceptance by relevant line managers that constitutes successful accomplishment of the job. This clearly tells the subordinate that part of his job is to do whatever is necessary not only to complete the report but also to ensure its acceptance.

The manager should specify the time frame within which he

expects the end result to be achieved. An objective could be expressed for any amount of time—a month, six months, a year. When the manager begins to consider termination, the objectives should permit ample opportunity to demonstrate improvement—usually four months or longer.

The important point is that the employee knows what the completion date is, so that the work effort does not drag on, mired in repeated arguments about how much progress is actually being made. When a final target date is established, it becomes possible for the manager and subordinate to identify benchmarks indicating how much progress has been made, and to assess whether or not the subordinate is making enough progress on the objective to be able to complete the job by the required date.

In summary, when dealing with a subordinate whose performance has not been effective in the past, setting exact objectives is an important part of the coaching process. These objectives should be expressed in terms of end-result orientation, specifying the extent to which an objective should be achieved and the time frame in which the job is to be completed.

The literature on MBO has always emphasized the importance of manager and subordinate agreeing on the objectives to be reached. Clearly, the extent to which there is mutual agreement about objectives influences the extent of how motivated a subordinate will be to reach these objectives. In practice, however, it is often difficult for a manager and subordinate to agree on which objectives are reasonable in terms of the resources the subordinate has available. Disagreements of this sort are even more likely when managers deal with subordinates whose past performances have been weak; these people are going to be threatened by the objective-setting process, and are probably already looking for excuses as to why their performance is not up to par.

To the extent that it is possible, the manager should make every effort to reach mutually acceptable goals. However, if after giving the matter conscientious thought and listening to the arguments the subordinate presents, the manager is convinced that the level of performance he is asking for is not unreasonable, the manager should not hesitate to insist upon the objectives he believes a capable person should have no trouble achieving.

In setting goals or objectives, the manager should call the subordinate in and state that he wishes to set specific performance criteria for a given period of time. The manager should make it clear that he considers it absolutely critical that the subordinate achieve these objectives.

If the manager is seriously displeased with the subordinate's past performance, this displeasure should have been recorded in recent performance appraisals. At the start of the goal-setting process, the manager should clearly indicate to the subordinate that, as they have previously discussed, his performance has not been up to standard. The manager should state that he wants to do everything possible to try to get the subordinate back into a position of making significant contributions to the work unit. As the first step in this process, he wants to make absolutely certain that the subordinate understands exactly what is expected of him and, for this reason, the manager wants to set specific objectives for the subordinate. The manager should note that it is absolutely critical for the subordinate to meet these objectives if he is to continue within the organization.

The manager should begin by outlining the objectives he feels the subordinate ought to reach. As he shares each objective with the subordinate, he should ask for the subordinate's reaction regarding whether or not the subordinate feels the objective is reasonable, what problems the subordinate expects to encounter in reaching the objective, and what advantages and resources the subordinate can bring to bear in meeting the objective.

During this part of the discussion, the manager should listen carefully to what the subordinate says. Based on what he hears, the manager should either make whatever adjustment is warranted or simply insist on the objective as he specified it to the subordinate. This conversation should be repeated for each of the objectives for which the subordinate will be held accountable.

The question often arises as to how many objectives the subordinate should have. In our experience, the rule of thumb should be that a few is better than too many. The objectives should be written for aspects of the job the manager regards as critical to the performance of the work unit. Once the subordinate starts getting overloaded with objectives, it becomes unreasonable to expect him to be able to accomplish all of them.

It is much more effective to emphasize key result areas in which the subordinate is expected to make a contribution. Also, in terms of trying to turn the subordinate's performance around, it is generally better to give the person a limited number of objectives that he or she can expect to reach than to weigh that subordinate down with an excessive number of objectives.

What do we mean by a few? Obviously, this is a discretionary type of thing, but in our experience about five or six is reasonable. In some instances, one or two is a reasonable number of objectives if they are, indeed, stretch objectives and represent a significant effort on the part of the subordinate. In other cases, six, seven, or eight may be warranted.

If the manager finds himself setting ten or more objectives, he should ask himself if he is really being reasonable in establishing all those objectives for the time period involved. Remember, once these objectives are set, they are going to be the primary measuring stick for determining whether or not the subordinate is improving his performance and whether termination is necessary.

Holding Frequent Progress Reviews

Frequent progress reviews accomplish three things: First, they serve as a continual reminder that reaching the objectives is important to the person's career with the organization. Without frequent reinforcement people often rationalize the fact that failure to meet their objectives could result in being fired.

Second, progress reviews provide an opportunity for the manager to recognize positive achievement toward objectives. If the subordinate is striving to meet his objectives, the manager can be supportive of his efforts. This can encourage further progress. Getting positive feedback is important to someone striving to improve his performance.

Third, if progress is not forthcoming, the manager can use the progress review to listen to the subordinate's reasons for his lack of performance and attempt to get him on track. In this sense, the review becomes a problem-solving session.

Whether or not the subordinate has made progress toward his objectives, holding frequent reviews permits the manager to remain in control of what is happening. At every review, the manager should discuss each of the objectives with the subordinate. The reason for progress or lack of it should be reviewed. Suggestions for improvement should be made.

The manager should take notes during these meetings so that he has a record of what was discussed. Hopefully, these will become a record of the subordinate's progress and development. If, however, the person fails to improve, these notes become a record of the manager's efforts at attempting to elicit improvement.

As long as the subordinate makes progress, the manager should be supportive. The focus of the conversation should be on the progress being made, with the manager emphasizing the positive. If, however, progress does not occur, the manager should be sure of doing three things:

1. Stating the downside of future failure. The manager should be sure to stress that failure to improve will result in termination.
2. Offering the upside of making progress. The manager

should continue to express hope that the person will improve, taking the objectives as an opportunity to demonstrate competence and a willingness to do the job.
3. Setting interim objectives the manager expects to be met by the next progress review. These interim objectives further clarify the progress expected and set up the next review discussion.

The progress reviews should continue until the person meets or misses his objectives or until it becomes clear the objectives cannot be reached in the remaining time.

The process outlined above is a thorough attempt at coaching the subordinate's performance. Unfortunately, in our experience, it seldom characterizes the year preceding a termination. All too often, it has been business as usual between boss and subordinate, until the boss decides he cannot take any more. Or objectives are set, but the boss doesn't follow through with the progress reviews. By taking the steps described above, a manager can be sure of being consistent with the policy guidelines suggested in Chapter 3.

Ideally, the coaching process results in improved performance, removing the need for termination. However, we live in a less than ideal world.

Chapter 6 discusses the termination process.

6

The Termination
Interview

NO MATTER HOW THOROUGH A COMPANY'S TER-
mination policy may be, it can be rendered largely
useless if managers do not conduct effective termination
interviews. It is the quality of the interpersonal process during the
interview that determines the impact of policy on the person being dismissed.

Let's be honest about it. There is no easy way to conduct the
interview. Firing someone is an unpleasant experience. Even
when the other person knows his past performance has been
poor, being let go is likely to generate defensiveness. Furthermore, very real economic and social problems confront the unemployed person. At the same time, the manager doing the firing
may feel he is playing God with the person's career. Most managers find this to be an unsettling feeling.

There is no way to make the termination interview a pleasant
experience. The goal is to make it as constructive as possible,
making sure the essential elements that need to be included in the
discussion are covered, and protecting the integrity of the company. A corollary to this is that the interview should proceed in a

way that minimizes the awkwardness for the manager doing the firing. Fortunately, there are skills that can be learned and procedures that can help achieve a calm, constructive interview.

Preparing for the Interview

Preparation is germane to effective termination interviews. Proper preparation helps the manager avoid the critical mistakes that typify spur-of-the-moment, angry terminations.

Our discussion of corporate policy in Chapter 3 and corrective coaching in Chapter 5 has suggested many of the critical elements of preparation. Prior to initiating a termination interview, the manager should already have had several conversations with the person about his poor performance. Unacceptable performance appraisals should have been given. Specific objectives toward which the employee is still failing to make progress should have been set and discussed.

The manager now wants to assemble the facts and documentation that justify the termination. He should be thoroughly familiar and comfortable with this material. The decision should be reviewed with the boss and the proper people in the personnel department, and the terms of the support package should be stated clearly in a letter.

Next, the manager can give his attention to the interview itself. Timing is an important consideration. If at all possible, the termination should be done early in the day at the beginning or middle of the week. Five o'clock on Friday is the worst possible time. The person being let go needs time to sort out what has happened to him and collect his thoughts, possibly asking questions of his contact within the company. Late-in-the-day and end-of-the-week terminations tend to preclude this, placing additional pressure on the employee, who has to go home before he is mentally prepared to face family and friends.

Nor should the termination take place just before the boss

goes on a trip, because it creates an impression of abandonment and retreat. While out of the office, the boss cannot respond to the reactions of others to the termination or to any unanticipated problems.

Still, a disproportionate number of terminations occur on Friday afternoon or before a business trip. A combination of procrastination on an unpleasant task and the desire to escape from the situation once the task is done seems to explain this preponderance of poor timing. The well-prepared manager avoids these timing errors.

The manager should prepare exactly how he plans to open the discussion. Thought should be given to the proper structuring of the interview. A model to help the manager in planning and conducting the interview is provided later in this chapter. Prior to meeting with the subordinate, the manager should have reviewed each step of the model.

In planning for the interview, the manager should anticipate how the employee might react. Being knowledgeable about the kinds of reactions experienced by people who are being terminated can help the manager avoid being caught off guard and misreading what is happening.

Understanding Reactions to Terminations

In preparing for the termination interview, it is helpful to visualize the type of reaction the employee might have to being terminated. Outplacement experts describe a range of reactions, most of which can be classified into one of the following five categories:

Anticipated Reactions

When the boss has done a good job of appraising past performance, the employee has been forewarned that his or her performance has not been consistent with management expectations. Then, many times, there is only a minimum level of surprise connected with the termination.

Managers should be cautioned, however, that even when they think they have done a good job of counseling the employee on what he or she has been doing wrong, the person is still shocked when the termination actually occurs. This happens for two reasons. First, even when the boss thinks performance problems are clearly delineated in performance appraisals, many times the more serious problems have been unconsciously downplayed in order to avoid unpleasantness. Therefore, the employee is still largely unaware of just how serious the problems are.

Second, even though the person has been told that problems exist, he or she may have blocked out the negative feedback or, in essence, avoided hearing what was said about inadequate performance. Also, many people tend to convince themselves that termination won't happen to them and, inevitably, when confronted with the reality of being let go, often feel some form of shock even though considerable dialogue about poor past performance had preceded the interview.

Nevertheless, when they have been repeatedly counseled about performance and know they've missed job assignments, many people are really aware of impending termination even if they seek to avoid recognizing it. In one unusual instance involving our firm, the person (Fred) was so sure he was going to be fired that he avoided coming into the office. Expecting to be terminated, Fred kept traveling or calling in sick. Eventually an outplacement consultant had to go to his home to talk to him and tell him he was being terminated.

This, of course, was an extreme case. However, since Fred would not show up at the office, the consultants (who were involved in the actual termination because of the somewhat bizarre circumstances) had to go to the employee's own turf to give him the news. As things turned out, there was not a great deal of trauma connected with the discussion. On the contrary, there was a certain amount of humor. Fred laughed about being a hard person to find; he said he knew he was going to be fired and he was just trying to postpone the inevitable. When the consultant arrived at his home, his family was out shopping and the whole interview went very smoothly. Fred was placed in a better position within three months.

Fortunately, not all anticipatory reactions are so extreme. However, they share certain characteristics with Fred's case. The person being terminated expects it is going to happen but hopes to delay it. Often, he will try to avoid the boss in the belief that staying out of sight will keep him out of the boss's mind. This person has actually accepted termination as inevitable so, typically, there is no dramatic effort made toward performance improvement.

When the termination occurs, this person will generally acknowledge that he expected it and, at times, will even seem relieved. Protest will be limited to statements that he still doesn't think it was entirely his fault or "It is a shame we couldn't work together." The interview typically proceeds in a straightforward, nonemotional way, with the terminated person concentrating on the particulars of the support package and other arrangements relating to the problem of what happens now.

Reactions of Total Disbelief

The antithesis of the person who anticipates being fired is the person who looks at the terminating manager in complete disbelief. This reaction is often characterized by the person saying nothing and looking as though he were in a state of shock.

Of all the reactions, this can be the most frightening to deal with. The boss needs to try to keep the conversation going as long as possible to draw out the individual. Some sort of reaction—perhaps negative, or at least accepting—needs to be elicited before the end of the interview. If the terminating manager cannot obtain a response of this type, an appropriate person in the personnel department should continue the discussion with the employee.

Management wants to avoid sending a person off in a state of disbelief, since he might do harm to himself. The person is not facing up to the reality of his situation. He hopes that if he stays quiet long enough, the nightmare will go away and he'll wake up. In essence, the manager needs to attempt to initiate dialogue with the employee until he talks about being fired.

John Fredericks is a typical example. John had worked with the company for 25 years and held so many different positions that he was known as a jack-of-all-trades and Mr. Company Man. After this length of service, one might imagine that he was well established with his superiors, peers, and subordinates. However, often management styles change within a company. John was caught in one of those sometimes inevitable situations in which his approach to the business was out of step with what was currently happening within the organization. Somehow, John didn't seem to be on the management team any more.

More specifically, John kept telling management that it was wrong in the way it handled certain business problems. Whether he was right or wrong in the long run will probably never be established. However, his superiors determined that he was no longer part of their team and could not be counted on or trusted to implement key programs with enthusiasm; therefore, he had to be dismissed.

In the termination interview, John was told very abruptly that he was being let go. The boss's exact words were "Your services are no longer needed." John's reaction was classic in terms of disbelief. He sat there and just stared at his boss. His only comment during the hour was "You can't do this to me; I won't allow it." John did respond with yes or no answers, but never engaged in any type of dialogue.

The company had not done a good job of documenting problems and counseling John prior to the termination interview. However, the day before the termination interview, it had arranged for outplacement counseling services to be made available to him by an outside firm. The counselor met with John immediately after the interview.

It took the outplacement consultant no less than six hours of counseling with John to get him to begin talking freely about his feelings and anxieties. Some of these anxieties centered around the fact that he did not know what to say to his friends or peers. After 25 years of service, money and advancement up the corporate ladder were no longer motivating him. Status and how people related to him, both on the job and in his community, were his primary concerns. John was deeply troubled about what to say to save face in the outside world and within the organization. The counselor dealt with his fears by helping John with a carefully worded explanation as to why he was changing careers and leaving the company.

The above case has several elements that are common to the disbelief reaction. A failure to document specific problems and review them systematically with the employee before firing him or her contributes to a climate in which dismissal is the farthest thing from the employee's mind. Couple this with a harsh or aggressive manner of breaking the news to the person, and conditions are created that intensify his or her disbelief. Although the case above was somewhat extreme, it typically takes a significant effort to get the discharged employee to talk. Therefore, the termination interview can last for a considerable length of time when a person reacts with disbelief.

Often, the interview itself needs to be supplemented by a skilled counselor. As we saw with John, the person usually is in shock over the threat that termination poses to some aspect of his or her life. Until the counselor succeeds in surfacing that threat and resolving it, the terminated person is unlikely to accept rationally the fact that he is being fired.

Lack of communication between management and the subordinate often leads to a reaction of disbelief, but adequate appraisals do not always preclude such a response. Many times people simply dismiss the possibility of being fired, believing that management will continue to tolerate them.

Jay, a training and development manager, persisted in organizing certain programs in the face of opposition from his immediate superior, the director of organization and manpower development. Jay was convinced that his approach was correct and believed it was his responsibility to proceed despite direction from his boss to the contrary. To make matters worse, Jay's style was considerably at odds with his superior's.

When his boss terminated him, Jay was shocked, although he had been warned that if the two couldn't get together on this thing, a change was going to be made. He kept saying that he was doing the job to the best of his ability.

At eleven-thirty that night, Jay's wife phoned his boss to ask if he knew where Jay was. Jay wasn't home and had not called. In fact, it was two days before Jay went home, still not sure what had happened or what to tell his family.

Euphoric Reactions

People with euphoric reactions respond in an upbeat, almost festive manner. They sound almost happy to be let go. They seem positive they can handle what is happening to them. The managers terminating them better believe this is not the case.

A person reacting this way is typically so geared to responding to the boss's direction that he is simply going along with being terminated just as he might go along with any other directive he received from a superior. In essence, the person is saying that whatever the boss wants is all right with him.

This person usually has no idea what the next step should be. Counselors often refer to people like him as disoriented. Many times they go and sit for days, even weeks, at their desks without making any preparations for leaving, even though they have been told that they are discharged.

Unfortunately, this disorientation can be intensified by the boss misreading the euphoric reaction. Relieved at the person's seeming acceptance of the situation, the boss often keeps the interview brief, focusing on the specifics of the termination package without paying any further attention to the psychological state of the individual who is being let go. Yet this person is exhibiting one of the reactions most in need of counseling support during the subsequent job search process.

One case that illustrates this reaction was that of a 37-year-old woman. She was referred to us by a corporate outplacement client who was terminating her. She seemed extremely happy about the situation. In fact, she was bubbly, excited, and really a pleasure to work with. It took her no less than two and a half years to find another position. In essence, nothing that was offered was interesting or real to her. On top of this, when she interviewed with potential employers, she created the impression of not being serious about finding a job.

Hence, her counselor had to keep trying to get her to calm down, to describe herself in business terms, and to set out clearly defined objectives in terms of finding her next job. It was a long, arduous process.

We have dealt with many cases like the one above, where those who are terminated can be classified as euphoric or in a state of feeling high. These are difficult people to work with because it is hard to bring them down to reality without crushing their spirit or hurting their drive. All terminated people go through cyclical periods of feeling high and low. They will get excited about the possibility of moving to a new job and then hit a low period in the job search process. The trouble with dealing with euphoric people is that they don't have the peaks and valleys of the normal candidate. They tend to stay on an unrealistic high. However, if they do come out of their euphoric state, they tend to crash into depression and are usually difficult to get back to a level at which they energetically look for a job.

Escapist Reactions

After an escapist type has been told that he is no longer with the company, he wants to leave the office immediately. Sometimes he will go back to the work unit and begin talking with others about the problems he is having with the boss or company.

The manager needs to try to retain this person in the office and initiate a dialogue on exactly why he is being let go. Every effort should be made to continue the discussion and help the person ventilate his feelings. It is important that the manager communicate the details of the support package. We know several instances when a person with this reaction has gone home and placed undue stress on his family because he left before understanding the terms of his termination. Typically, the boss let him leave, relieved that the problem seemed to be over.

It's helpful if a personnel officer can spend some time with this person after the interview with the manager is over. The personnel officer can get the terminated employee off the premises, go out and have a cup of coffee with him or her, and continue to discuss that person's feelings. If this is not done, the escapist is most likely to ventilate to others—co-workers, family, other people in the industry, perhaps even the press.

Violent Reactions

The violent person overreacts to the situation by screaming, hollering obscenities, or even threatening physical harm to himself, the company, or the person who is terminating him. The objective of the manager should be to allow that person to ventilate his feelings. Rather than argue with the person or defend the company, the manager should ask questions. Why does he feel he is being mistreated? How could his career have been handled differently? Eventually, the person will quiet down as he talks about his situation.

But even after he has calmed down, this person may continue to make threats about what he will do to get back at the company. Often, he will talk in terms of a lawsuit or going public with embarrassing information. The manager should not get defensive, but continue to listen to the employee and ask questions. Above all, the manager must avoid making promises to him or her, with such statements as: "We will try to do something for you," or "I'll help you find a job." Such remarks reinforce the person's belief that he has been mistreated.

Any time a person being terminated threatens a legal action, the manager should simply acknowledge that it is the subordinate's right to do so. However, the manager should state firmly that he believes the documentation will support management's contention that it was within its rights in discharging the employee. In short, the manager should recognize the employee's right to pursue legal recourse without encouraging it. Basically, he should listen. If the policy and the guidelines within this book are followed, the company has little to fear from litigation.

One of us was involved in a situation in which the terminated employee threatened to shoot his boss. After a period of outplacement consultation, he even threatened physical harm to the counselor. Such cases are rare, however. In fact, violent verbal reactions occur in only a distinct minority of instances. Usually, the terminating manager is needlessly anxious about a violent overreaction on the part of the subordinate.

Actually, the violent person who is striking out at the moment—ranting and raving—is ventilating his or her anger. A day or two later, after having time to think about the situation, he or she usually realizes it is not going to do any good to go out and do something that is likely to render him or her unemployable or even result in legal problems. The person then begins to channel his anger into productive endeavors. This is exactly what happened to the person described in the preceding paragraph. He used his hostility to good advantage by being very energetic and creative in his job search.

The above kinds of reactions have been experienced by almost all outplacement specialists. Trained as counselors and experienced in dealing with people bei̶ ▓▓▓▓▓ed, they are capable of recognizing how the person is reacting and retaining their poise and continuing the interview. For the line manager, the problem is somewhat more severe. Under the pressure of the termination interview, it is easy to become defensive and to forget to analyze what is happening and control the conversation. When a company designates a specialist in the personnel department to assist the manager, the likelihood of adequate follow-through increases, since the specialist is more familiar with termination than other managers and thus has become more adept at handling them.

Review of the possible reactions should be part of the preparation of any manager about to initiate a termination discussion. In the interview itself the manager should remember the following guidelines:

- Continue the interview until the person appears to be talking freely and reasonably calmly about the reasons for his termination and the support package.
- Try to avoid becoming defensive about the termination. Encourage the person to talk.
- Beware of any reaction in which acceptance, either passive or enthusiastic, seems to lead to almost immediate conclusion of the interview.
- Try to avoid letting the person storm out of the office.
- Don't make any promises or apologies. Stick to the content of the support package.

The manager should commit these guidelines to memory, so that he can remain in control of the interview regardless of the person's reaction.

What to Cover in the Interview

It is absolutely critical that the terminated person understand why he is being terminated, and that the decision is final. As we have stressed repeatedly, the manager should establish at least three, preferably more, reasons the termination is occurring. He should stick to these reasons, no matter what the subordinate's reaction. This is not a counseling session in which the manager is obligated to listen openmindedly for the possibility that he will hear something that might change his assessment of the situation. Such discussions have preceded the decision to discharge the person. Rather, the purpose of the interview is to tell the employee about a nonreversible decision. The manager is listening in order to help the subordinate accept the decision, not to surface new information.

The problems should all have been discussed before. Even if the subordinate does not accept the manager's reasoning, the only proper position for the manager is "Well, I'm sorry that we disagree. However, I think it is important that you at least know why we are terminating you and how we saw your performance."

Above all, the manager should avoid giving fictitious reasons for the termination. This may seem obvious, yet it is amazing how often managers give reasons that are easier to sell to the person than his own lack of performance. We encountered one person who had been let go three times in five years. No one had given him serious feedback on his problems, and he was under the impression that he had bad luck in choosing jobs. His outplacement counselor was the first one to help him identify and work out his problems.

People need to know why they were fired; otherwise they have no opportunity to avoid making the same mistakes in the future. Giving them concrete reasons helps them digest what went wrong. Management does a person a severe disservice by not giving specific reasons.

Also, there should be no question but that the decision is final. Throughout the interview, the manager should make it clear that the issue facing the subordinate is "What do I do next?" and not "How do I get my job back?" The manager should be especially careful neither to apologize for the termination nor to promise to see what else is available in the company. These are common mistakes that tend to cloud the issue, and often lead the person to believe that he has a chance to save his job. The manager's posture should be, "We have discussed these problems before and management has already looked at the option of placing you elsewhere in the company. Our decision is that it is in the best interest of both of us for you to go elsewhere."

Along these same lines, never suggest that the company (or the manager) will help the person find another job. Remember, a major hurdle most people must clear when they are terminated is to get moving and look for work. Well-intended efforts at softening the blow by promising to help out tend to delay the acceptance of the new situation by the terminated employee. Thus, such efforts are really more damaging than helpful. A cardinal rule is that *the manager should not make any commitments to help the person beyond those contained in the support package.*

It is important that the support package be discussed and understood. This is a critical part of the interview. The manager should make an outline of the support package before the interview and then refer to his notes to be sure each point is reviewed with the person being terminated.

Once the appropriate preparations have been made, the problem is one of execution of the interview. It is helpful if the manager has a model to help him structure the ensuing discussion.

A Model for Conducting the Termination Interview

Terminating someone is difficult; no gimmicks or tricks can make it pleasant or easy. However, experience indicates that managers tend to make certain mistakes during the interview that create unnecessary difficulties for either the manager doing the termination or the person being let go. To the extent that a manager can avoid these mistakes, the termination interview is more likely to go smoothly. Even more importantly, the manager is less likely to jeopardize the company's legal position.

Below we suggest a model or approach for handling the termination interview. The sequencing of the steps is important, since getting out of sequence can undermine the effectiveness of the discussion. Furthermore, underlying each step are certain skills and procedures that can facilitate the interview. It is especially worth the manager's time to develop these skills, since many of them are applicable to a variety of other managerial situations as well. In this sense, they are general management skills.

Step 1. Get to the point.
Step 2. Describe the situation.
Step 3. Listen:
  • Open-ended questions
  • Restatement
  • Expanders
  • Silence
Step 4. Discuss the severance package.
Step 5. Identify the next step.

Step 1. Get to the Point

When terminating someone, managers often find it difficult to get to the point. Frequently, they are so evasive that it is several minutes before the subordinate begins to realize what is happening to him. An opening such as, "Would you like a cup of coffee? I don't know how. . . . How is it going on the line?" is representative of how the conversation often gets initiated.

Managers frequently make small talk about the kids, last weekend's big game, the state of the economy, or some remote topic in an effort to delay the actual firing. This small talk is often rationalized as an effort toward placing the subordinate at ease. Of course, the real reason for the small talk is the manager's uneasiness. Uncomfortable, perhaps even a little fearful, the manager is still seeking to put off the inevitable.

Sometimes, the manager attempts to ease in through an indirect approach. Thus he begins by making indirect comments such as "Things haven't been going well lately," or "How do you feel about the job you have been doing?" Subconsciously, the manager is hoping the person will take the hint and quit. Unfortunately, all too often the person seizes the initiative by voicing a strong desire to improve or asking how he can do better. Now the manager is in a bind, since he has to state that doing better is no longer an option; the person is being fired.

For example, a partner in a large public accounting firm was given the task of terminating a staff person whose performance did not merit continued association with the firm. The partner began by stating that the staff person's evaluation on his last job was not good. The staff person responded that he was not satisfied with his performance either and hoped to do better on the next engagement. Next, the partner commented that this had not been the first time that his job performance was rated as inadequate or below average. At this point, the staff person stated that he, too, had been concerned with how his career was going and was glad that someone in the firm was finally going to sit down and have a thorough discussion with him about what he could do in order to improve his performance. At this point, the partner got exceedingly uncomfortable and suggested that they both give it some thought and that perhaps the staff member ought to talk to the partner in charge of the office.

A basic principle of counseling is that the more severe the problem the more important it is to avoid manufactured small talk and get to the point. Terminating someone is one of the most severe counseling situations. Therefore, it is imperative to get directly to the point. The longer the manager procrastinates, the greater the false atmosphere that is created, making it more awkward to present the real purpose of the meeting. Furthermore, the longer the manager delays in telling the subordinate the true purpose of the discussion, the more chance there is that the conversation will take a turn that puts the manager on the defensive.

When the subordinate enters the manager's office, the manager should give him a moment to get comfortable, then should inform the subordinate of his decision.

Step 2. Describe the Situation

The manager's uneasiness about the termination interview can lead to an overkill situation in which the manager seemingly wants to devastate the person being let go. Apprehension that the person will resist the termination often leads the manager to decide that a good offense is the best defense. The result is an unnecessarily brutal termination. Other times a manager will be exceedingly vague about the termination, so much so that it is not even clear that the person is being dismissed. One approach is as bad as the other.

In informing the subordinate of the termination decision, the manager should describe the situation, not attack the person. In doing so, he should be very specific. The interview should begin with a statement similar to:

> John, I am really very sorry but I am going to have to let you go. Production in your area is down 4 percent, and we are continuing to have quality problems. Several of your supervisors are still unaware of key operating procedures. We have talked about these problems several times in the past three months, and the solutions are not being followed through. We have to make a change.

Or perhaps the opening might go like this:

> John, I have to let you go. In the past, we have talked about the inconsistencies in how our policies are being followed out in the shop. Yesterday, you failed to discipline two of your people for being 15 minutes late from lunch. People are talking instead of working, and attendance remains a problem. I have to make a change.

What do both of these illustrations have in common? First, the manager begins by informing the subordinate of the termination decision. Sometimes a subordinate will interrupt at this point and ask why. Usually, however, he will listen, somewhat in a state of shock. In either event, the manager should continue. As we saw in the above examples, the manager describes the situation or situations that led to the decision. These are stated in very specific terms. The manager gives at least three illustrations of the problem and reminds the person that these have been discussed repeatedly in the past. Finally, the manager reaffirms the decision to terminate the employee.

Notice that the manager does not attack the subordinate personally. Comments such as "You are too careless" or "Your lack of effort is responsible for your removal" have been avoided. These are judgments about the person's character that are virtually impossible for him to accept. They are also highly subjective judgments that can be difficult to defend. For example, stating that someone has "exhibited almost total disregard for our reporting system" is going to generate considerable defensiveness, certainly much more than the comment "During the last six months your management report has been at least three days late." The latter is the objective basis for the termination.

Descriptive statements are more effective because they make it easier for the person to focus on the reasons he or she is being terminated. They avoid the additional, unnecessary conflict generated by evaluative inferences on the motivation behind the poor performance.

Stating things descriptively is a learnable communication skill. With practice any manager can do it effectively. In preparing a descriptive opening, the manager can use the following questions as guidelines:

What are the actual events that led to the termination decision? What has the manager actually observed, measured, or experienced regarding the reasons for the subordinate's termination? If the reasons are performance based, it is obviously helpful for the manager to be able to refer to specific performance objectives. Regardless of why the individual is being terminated, the manager should be able to present specific occurrences. For example: "Reports have been late." "Production has not improved to agreed-upon levels." "You have received three poor performance appraisals."

Even integrity problems can be presented descriptively. For example: "You reported that you visited our distributors in the northeast section of the state. Subsequently, they inquired as to when you were going to visit them since they have not seen any of our people for over six months." Or "You reported that you audited our inventory figures, but the data were never collected."

All the examples have focused on actual occurrences, thus providing a substantive basis for the termination.

How frequently have the problems been observed? How many reports have been late or how long has production been below acceptable levels? How many complaints have been received? When the manager can specify the number of times problems have been observed, the statement becomes even more descriptive and substantive. Thus, the manager can state: "Five times in the last six months, your monthly management reports have been late by more than a week. . . . On three occasions, we discussed this problem."

Notice that the above example states both the frequency of the occurrence of the problem and the number of times the manager and subordinate have already discussed it. Stating the frequency with which the problems have been discussed in the past helps to specify the seriousness of the problem further.

What, if any, were the observable consequences? In considering this question, the manager is attempting to identify what additional problems have been created by the subordinate's actions. For example, perhaps the failure to do timely review of a parts inventory has led to stalled progress for resolving parts shortages on the production floor. Or perhaps several key customer accounts have complained about the lack of responsiveness to their problems.

By answering these three guideline questions, a manager will develop specific descriptive statements that inform the subordinate, without any personal attack, why he or she is being let go. At the same time, the employee will have no doubt about the purpose of the interview.

To summarize, the manager should get directly to the point in a descriptive fashion. In fact, *the termination should take place in the first five minutes of the interview*. Once this is done, the manager's concern can focus on the subordinate's reaction.

Step 3. Listen

No matter how descriptive the opening is, the most likely reaction will be one of shock, disbelief, or defensiveness. As we discussed earlier in this chapter, these reactions can take a variety of forms. For the manager, the most important thing is to *avoid arguing* with the person.

The first priority is to get the subordinate talking as much as possible about the termination. This is because:

• The more the subordinate talks, the easier it is for the manager to determine which of the many possible reactions the subordinate is having to being discharged.

• Getting the subordinate to discourse in a relatively calm fashion is basic to ensuring that he has a reasonable understanding of his current position. Sometimes getting him to talk will be easy.

For example, with either the euphoric or violent reaction, the subordinate typically expresses himself verbally. Other times, this task will be harder. Disbelief and escapism are two reactions in which the person may not express himself other than by shaking his head or seeming only to want to leave the office.

When a subordinate reacts verbally, the manager's principal

concern should be to listen, encouraging the person to express his feelings as a first step toward focusing on the reality of the situation. Counselors call this ventilation. The manager's principal problems are to avoid becoming defensive and to avoid saying something that might undermine the objective rationale for terminating the individual.

For example, if the subordinate begins to blame his failure on the manager, it is easy for the manager to become upset and begin making highly evaluative and subjective comments about the subordinate, comments that are not germane to the objective reasons for the firing. Such statements not only inflame the conversation but also undermine the entire termination process. They provide fuel for the subordinate's belief that he was treated unfairly, that the boss had it in for him. For these reasons, it is important that the boss minimize his input while letting the subordinate talk.

If, however, a subordinate closes up, the manager's problem becomes one of drawing him out. Here the boss has to use interpersonal skills to get the subordinate talking about the situation; only by talking about the situation is the person likely to come to terms with why he is being fired.

Certain core communication skills are particularly applicable during this step of the model. Specifically, these skills are:

- Open-ended questions
- Restatement
- Expanders
- Silence

Open-ended questions. An open-ended question is a question that cannot easily be answered with a yes or no. Open-ended questions begin with the word "what," "how," "where," or "when." In contrast, close-ended questions are easily answered in a yes or no fashion. Close-ended questions typically begin with the words "can," "do," "did," "are," "has," "would," and "could."

Because open-ended questions cannot easily be answered

with a yes or no, they generally elicit a broader response from another person. Apart from this, open-ended questions minimize defensiveness on the part of the other person. Close-ended questions tend to force the other person into a position of deciding whether he wants to come down on the positive or negative side of the yes/no question. This decision can be threatening. Often the person feels that the question has boxed him into a corner. Open-ended questions make it easier for the other person to explain his position.

For these reasons, open-ended questions are generally more effective during the exploration stage of a sensitive discussion with another person. They are particularly effective when trying to get the subordinate to discuss his reaction to being terminated. Asking questions such as the following can help generate constructive dialogue with the person:

"What were your reactions when last month's figures showed no improvement?"

"How did you feel after our last talk about this problem?"

"When during the last six months did things look as if they were turning around?"

"In retrospect, what could you have done differently?"

The questions should be linked directly to the subordinate's situation. The point of this step is not to generate idle conversation, but to help him talk about what happened.

Unfortunately, most questions that get asked in our society are close-ended. Listen to the questions that are asked during conversations in the office. You'll see that most of them are phrased in a close-ended fashion. This is fine for casual conversation, but gets in the way of effective management of tense boss/subordinate communications. The problem for the manager in learning to use open-ended questions is to overcome old habits. One way to do this is consciously to practice phrasing questions in an open-ended fashion until the skill is developed.

Restatement. Restatement is another of the core listening skills. Essentially, restatement is the practice of rephrasing a key point the subordinate has just made. This does several things. First, it allows the subordinate to react to his own thoughts and ideas without having to argue with the boss. Second, it is an expression of interest and understanding on the boss's part that encourages the subordinate to share more of his feelings. Thus, restatement tends to facilitate the discussion in a nonadversary fashion. Finally, when the subordinate is upset and verbally attacking the boss, restating can help the manager to avoid a defensive reaction. For example:

Subordinate	I tried my hardest. We both agreed that a joint effort was going to be required. I don't think I ever got full support for my program.
Manager	(restating) Under the circumstances, you feel you have done everything possible.
Subordinate	Certainly. For example. . . .

Notice how restatement helps the manager to respond to the subordinate's accusation of lack of support in a nondefensive manner while encouraging the subordinate to continue to ventilate his feelings.

Restatement is best used when the subordinate is emotionally involved in what he is saying. Under these conditions, restatement is a nonobtrusive way of helping the subordinate express his feelings. It is one of the most useful of listening skills; it is also one of the most difficult to learn. Therefore, as with open-ended questions, conscious practice is required, prior to participating in a termination interview, if a manager is to become skilled in using this technique.

Expanders. As the subordinate is talking, the manager should express interest and understanding in what is being said. Little gestures such as maintaining good eye contact, occasionally nodding the head, and verbal expressions such as "Uh huh" and "I see" help relax the person and encourage the discussion.

These gestures are referred to as expanders because that is

what they do; they encourage the person to expand on his comments.

Silence. It goes without saying that if the object of this step of the model is to listen, the manager should be as silent as possible, yet in our experience, this is easier to say than to do in a termination interview. The tension and nervousness that characterize the conversation tend to result in most managers talking too much. In an effort to control the conversation, they dominate it. In the process, they undermine the effectiveness of the termination interview.

There are two ways in which silence can be used effectively. One is right after asking a question. All too often, managers continue talking after asking a question, suggesting the answer they want to hear, asking additional questions, or even going off on another train of thought. This, of course, defeats the purpose of asking questions in the first place. It really is a skill to ask a question and pause, waiting for an answer. Our advice to managers is to be aware of how often you do this and strive to improve.

Silence is equally helpful after the other person has been talking. Often a pause, accompanied by an expectant look, will result in the person continuing to talk. Simply giving the person an opportunity to expand on what he has been saying is one of the most effective of listening techniques. Once again, the tendency to dominate the conversation can defeat this simple, but important, listening technique.

Managers should remember that the termination interview is not a problem-solving session. The time for that approach between boss and subordinate was in the months preceding the termination decision. Any further attempts at identifying the cause of the problem implies that perhaps another chance is in order. In the absence of extraordinary new information, such a consideration at this point in the process is not only inappropriate but virtually almost always ineffective. We should be able to assume that the manager has done his homework, previous solutions have failed, and the manager is firm in his conviction that a change is necessary. If any questions exist, the manager should not have proceeded this far with the termination process.

In response to the employee's questions, the manager should state that the decision regarding the termination is final, the problems have been discussed before, and the employee needs to be most concerned about what he is going to do next. For example, consider the following exchange:

Subordinate	Look, I don't think anyone can do the job better. I have been working hard on the problems. I know the operation like the back of my hand. This doesn't make any sense.
Manager	John, the decision to make the change has been made. For nine months we have been meeting at least once a week on this matter. Whether or not someone else can succeed remains to be seen, but I feel it is our best approach to make a change at this time. You need to be concerned about the future, not the past. Make sure your next move is a good one.
Subordinate	Frank, this thing requires time. I wish I could get you to see that. Don't be unreasonable.
Manager	(using restatement) You feel that with time the problems would be resolved; that we are treating you unreasonably.
Subordinate	Hell, yes. Remember, I have a lot at stake here too.
Manager	I think your feelings are natural, but I also think we are doing the right thing. Time will tell. You need to be thinking about your next step now.

Notice that in the above dialogue the manager is not arguing with John. Rather, he is focusing attention on the fact that problems do exist and that other things that have been tried have not resolved them, and he is confirming the decision that has been made to let John go. In doing this, he reiterates that John needs to be planning ahead to find his next job.

In conducting the interview, there is nothing wrong with allowing the subordinate to talk about what he might have done differently as long as the manager does not imply he might have another chance at the job. The posture should be one of agreeing that hindsight can be useful to future efforts. Discussing the problems of the past can also help the subordinate realize that perhaps a change is warranted and is in his best interest as well as the company's.

The goal of the listening step is to get the subordinate to talk freely about the situation and to recognize that his immediate concern is the future, not his former job.

Sometimes, after ventilating his feelings, the subordinate will focus on the issues himself. "Well, right or wrong, my problem is what happens now. Are you just throwing me out on the street?" This is one posture that might be adopted by the employee.

Other times, the manager can facilitate this process by summarizing the conversation. "Although we disagree on whether this is the correct solution, it is the one I have made. Let's talk about what happens next." That is one way to help the interview along. "Accepting the decision I have made, what problems do you have?" This is another approach, and one that is often effective when a person is experiencing disbelief. Such a person often has specific concerns that need to be dealt with before he can accept the fact that he has been fired.

Obviously, none of these approaches is a substitute for more thorough counseling, which can help the person to understand what went wrong and what his future problems might be. More specific help in thinking through what went wrong is best done by a third-party outplacement specialist. Obviously, the manager and subordinate have not been able to resolve their problems in the past. It is most unlikely that the termination interview will result in any new insights.

Remember, *the purpose of the termination interview is not*

counseling. Rather, it is to communicate the decision that has been made and, as much as possible, to encourage the employee to accept it. If at all possible, the subordinate should leave the interview recognizing that his energies need to be directed toward finding new employment and understanding his exact status with his former employer.

Step 4. Discuss the Severance Package

Once the subordinate seems prepared to discuss the fact that he is being let go, the manager should carefully review all elements of his support package. It is best for the manager to outline the points he wants to cover before the interview begins. In this way, he can be sure that important areas are not omitted.

Severance payments, benefits, access to office support people, and how recommendations will be handled should all be explained. It goes without saying that the manager should answer any questions about the specifics of the package. However, *no promises or benefits beyond those already in the support package should be implied.*

If the subordinate tries to negotiate other arrangements, the manager should simply state that the package cannot be negotiated. The manager should avoid promising to look into something and get back to the subordinate at a later date. This puts him in a position of obligation that further complicates the termination process.

If, after the pressure of the interview is over, the manager feels that something can legitimately be added to the support package, he can always discuss it with the appropriate company officials and, if it is approved, notify the former employee. However, the manager should avoid setting up such obligations during the termination interview. This is important, since managers often are inclined to make promises to soften the interview.

The only exception should be when the manager cannot answer questions about a specific point in the support package.

Then the manager should make a note of the question and tell the employee the company will get back to him. At the conclusion of this step, the manager gives the terminated subordinate the letter spelling out the support package that is being provided.

Step 5. *Identify the Next Step*

When someone has been terminated, he is often disoriented and unsure of what to do next. He may panic and begin calling all his contacts before he has thought through what he is going to say to them about his career plans and why he is making a change. This, of course, is a mistake that may cause the contacts to duck future calls now that they are alerted that he needs a job.

There is also the awkward question of where the subordinate goes next. Does he go back to his desk for the day, clean it out and leave, or simply leave the premises and have his personal things forwarded to him?

These problems point up the advantages of having the employee meet with an outplacement specialist immediately upon leaving the manager's office. The specialist can help the subordinate deal with his feelings in a way that, because of the nature of the situation, the boss cannot.

Meeting with an outplacement counselor in a private location gives the person a place to go to collect his thoughts and plan his next step. He can decide whether to get his belongings and determine what he is going to tell his family. He can begin planning what he is going to do the next morning. Because of the critical nature of these hours following the termination interview, we strongly suggest that the person have an opportunity to meet with such a specialized counselor, one who is prepared to help him with his predicament.

When such help is available, the manager can indicate that the company is providing such assistance at no cost to the terminated employee and that the counselor is prepared to meet with him. The employee almost always accepts the counseling. The manager can then introduce him to the outplacement specialist. Specifics on the outplacement role, including how the introduction should be handled, are presented in Chapter 8.

In the absence of such counseling resources, the manager is less able to facilitiate the employee's next step. However, three points should be emphasized:

1. *Discuss where the employee should go upon leaving the manager's office.* This should be discussed in some detail, since the person is most likely to be confused about what happens now. We suggest that the manager give the employee the option of leaving immediately or remaining for the day and organizing his personal things. Most people opt to spend a few hours collecting their possessions and their thoughts before leaving the office.

Forcing the employee off the premises does little good for the company or the individual, and does not sit well with peers when they hear of it. Forget about waxing eloquent on the subject of teamwork after having a security person escort a former member of the team down to the street. Still, this is how many organizations handle terminated people.

2. *Remind the person of his company contact.* Repeat the name of the person the terminated employee should contact with any questions that might come up about either the support package or references. Be sure he knows whom he can contact—this provides a minimum level of psychological support.

3. *Advise the person to avoid precipitous action.* Suggest that the person collect his thoughts and develop an action plan before getting in touch with friends and valuable industry contacts. Remind him that his support package means that he will not starve as of tomorrow. Encourage him to consider his options, develop a résumé along with a job search plan, and *then* start making it known that he is available. Beyond these considerations, there is little the manager can do. At this stage, the interview should be ended.

The termination interview is always difficult; however, the above approach can make it as professional as possible. A sample worksheet that can help a manager prepare for and structure the termination interview is shown on the following page.

A question we are often asked is: "What if the manager can't do it?" Sometimes the organization feels that the boss is likely to lose control of the termination interview. Perhaps he or she is overly apprehensive about the termination. Or the boss may have been close to the subordinate on a social level and just can't deal with the issue. Personal biases might make it easy for the manager to lose self-control. In the final analysis, managers are seldom hired for their termination skills.

If the organization feels the manager is unlikely to be effective in the termination interview or the manager feels he or she can't do it, either the manager's superior or a personnel specialist should sit in on the interview. In effect, the two of them should conduct the interview as a team.

The manager of the person being terminated should always be present. This is the person who should initiate and attempt to carry the principal burden of the interview. The other person is present to give support and to be certain the termination occurs in a clearly communicated fashion.

WORKSHEET FOR PREPARING A TERMINATION INTERVIEW

Before the interview, fill out this worksheet to help you prepare yourself.

1. How many discussions have been held with the employee about the problem?_____Are they documented?_____

2. How many negative performance appraisals exist?_____

3. Has the termination been discussed by management and personnel?_____

4. Has a letter describing the support package been written?_____ Do you have an outline of the key elements of the support package?_____

5. Have you reviewed the possible reactions?_____

6. GET TO THE POINT. Opening line:_____

_____

_____

_____

7. DESCRIBE THE SITUATION. Three examples: What events are causing the termination? How frequently have they been observed? What were the observable consequences?_____

_____

_____

_____

7

Outplacement
Counseling

FOR THE PERSON WHO IS DISMISSED, THE TERMI-
nation interview is the beginning of a personal ordeal.
Searching for work can be one of the most ego-deflating
experiences in life. Unfortunately, this ordeal is intensified by
a lack of knowledge about the job search process. Mistakes
and lost opportunities unnecessarily extend the period of unemployment. If the person has difficulties of a personal nature, the
problems are compounded. Thus, many companies are coming
to recognize the need to provide systematic support past the
termination interview. Increasingly, companies are looking to
outplacement counseling as a vehicle for providing this support.

What Is Outplacement Counseling?

Outplacement counseling (OPC) is a systematic process by which
a terminated person is trained and counseled in the techniques of
self-appraisal and securing new employment appropriate to his
needs and talents. Contrary to popular misconception, outplacement counseling does not assume responsibility for placing the

terminated person in a new job. Rather, it is truly a counseling service. Its purpose is to provide the person with advice, instruction, and a sounding board that can help him in organizing and executing the job search.

We hope that by now the possible value of such counseling is evident to the reader. The pyramid shown here presents a step-by-step approach to obtaining a new job. A multitude of questions can emerge in a person's mind as he wrestles with each step in the process. Indeed, awareness of a systematic step-by-step approach, as shown in the figure on the following page, is often a major contribution of the OPC process.

Organizing an Outplacement Program

Establishment of an outplacement program represents an extension of the termination specialist's role discussed in Chapter 3. All the activities and characteristics discussed in that chapter are pertinent here as well. However, as a company moves into providing complete outplacement support, it must consider additional organizational issues.

Using Consultants or In-House Specialists

In deciding whether to offer outplacement counseling as part of the severance support package, a basic decision has to be made on whether to use outside consultants or internal specialists. As with any managerial service, there are advantages and disadvantages associated with either option.

If competent, external consultants are usually experienced in a wide range of industries. In many companies they enjoy a level of credibility that is not afforded to the internal specialist. As one personnel director remarked: "The history of this company is such that involvement of consultants is a signal that a new program is being taken seriously by management."

When handling sensitive outplacements, consultants are of-

ten able to get management to agree to certain conditions that an internal specialist might suggest but be reluctant to push. Furthermore, since the external outplacement consultant is not an employee of the company, it is often easier for him to obtain the confidence of the person receiving the counseling service. He can be viewed as being less biased in the whole process.

Internal specialists, on the other hand, can certainly establish considerable respect for their expertise within an organization, and there are specific advantages to internal specialists. An internal specialist is readily available to respond to the needs of the organization. Working in the company, he can often spot problem areas in termination practices that might elude an outside consultant.

Usually, establishing internal expertise places more emphasis on the establishment and maintenance of corporate termination policy in advance of the termination interview. Unfortunately, outside consultants are seldom retained much before the actual termination is to occur. Thus, they are in a position to have only minimal impact on the events that preceded the decision to let the person go.

Many companies use a combination of internal and external specialists. The internal specialists develop and maintain corporate policy in this area, often in collaboration with outside consultants. They also handle much of the OPC work within the corporation. Their external consultants are employed for special cases, such as the termination of very senior managers or someone with a particular problem.

A word about the costs of OPC services. Most outplacement counseling firms charge from 15 to 25 percent of the terminated person's compensation level. This fee is collected in return for providing a specific set of services. The details of these services vary from firm to firm, but any complete outplacement service will include the elements in this chapter. Consulting on company policy and procedures is typically billed on a per-diem basis, usually $750 to $1,000 a day.

OPC Is Part of the Support Package

Whether internal or external experts are used, an outplacement program should be conceived as being part of the support package offered to a person being terminated. Essentially, the manager doing the termination should explain to the person that the company provides the service should he choose to use it. Use of the OPC should have no bearing on the financial benefits of the support package. These should remain the same regardless of whether or not the person accepts the counseling. In our experience, virtually everyone chooses to use it.

The manager holding the termination interview should describe the general scope of the outplacement services at the conclusion of the termination interview. A counselor should be available to meet with the dismissed person immediately after the interview. Thus, the next step after the termination interview is getting together with the OPC counselor.

The availability of OPC takes some of the pressure off the manager doing the termination. Since he knows that counseling is available, he is less likely to make ill-advised promises of help or similar mistakes. When professional support is available, managers are almost always more forthright in the interview. Furthermore, the next step becomes a structured one—meeting the counselor—and therefore less awkward. Finally, the counselor can pick up where the manager leaves off in helping the person think through or ventilate his feelings about the company. Thus, OPC is particularly relevant for the more difficult reactions such as avoidance; reactions the average manager is unlikely to penetrate during the termination interview.

Who Is the Client?

For the outplacement counselor to be effective, he must be aware of whom he is serving. The person being terminated must be the client throughout the counseling process. The company terminating the employee is *sponsoring* the service in the sense that it is absorbing the expense of providing the counseling. However, the counselor's primary professional responsibility is to the person being dismissed in all matters that pertain to his particular termination and job search. He is the recipient of the service.

One of the counselor's first tasks is to clarify this relationship with the person being let go. For the counseling process to be effective, it is important that the person have complete trust that the counselor's advice and suggestions are intended solely for his benefit.

For example, one outplacement client harbored the belief that the counselor's job was in part to be supportive of the company's reasons for terminating him. Thus, he continually resisted feedback from the counselor regarding personal characteristics that might hinder his job search. Most of the counselor's suggestions were met by a shaking of the head and quiet resistance.

Finally, the person shot back: "Look, you have to say that because they are paying you to." At this point, counselor and client confronted the issue head on. After a half hour of discussion, the matter was resolved. Things went more smoothly in subsequent sessions.

Another client suspected that the counselor's job was to direct him away from certain competitors. Once again, the depth of his suspicions only became evident after a couple of meetings with the counselor. When the counselor realized that the person was remaining remote and distant, and had little enthusiasm for what they were discussing, the counselor confronted the person directly, saying, "I don't feel that you are convinced this process will help you. Let's talk about how you feel toward what we're doing here."

Initially, the counselee responded by stating that he was enthusiastic about the process. However, when the counselor stated again that his reactions seemed to suggest otherwise, the person said, "Look, some of your ideas make sense, but you're working for the company, and I have to watch out for my own best interests." In the ensuing discussion, it became clear that the person felt the counselor was advising him to consider a range of alternative career possibilities in a covert effort to steer him away from the competition.

Once the problem was on the table, the counselor pointed out how many people in similar jobs move from his company to the competition every year (and vice versa). His company had little to gain by attempting to influence his job search, and if it had, more direct methods, such as placing his previous performance in the harshest possible light, would be more likely to work. Gradually, the person came to trust his counselor.

Usually, any problem of this nature can be resolved during the initial meeting as long as the counselor is careful to clarify his role and to answer any questions in a straightforward manner. However, an outplacement counselor needs to be sensitive to the need for establishing a relationship of trust between himself and the person being terminated. When a terminated employee is especially paranoid about his former company, an outside outplacement counselor frequently has the edge in gaining the person's confidence, simply because he is not an employee of the corporation.

Such suspicions are often fueled by the terminated person's imagination. Having been rejected, he often rationalizes that the company needs to protect itself from him. Seeing himself as someone who can come back to haunt the company and thus reveal the blunder that was made in firing him is a source of psychological comfort, as well as an emotional outlet for hostility.

The counselor's job is to enable the person to move beyond such nonrational beliefs and channel the hostility into constructive action—finding a job in which he can succeed. For this relationship to work, the client must be the one receiving the service, and the counselor's efforts must be directed toward that person's best interests.

Of course, in areas of policy and practice, as well as in the counseling of managers on how to terminate, the outplacement counselor does have a client relationship with management. But once the counselor meets with the person being terminated he must shift his primary consulting responsibilities to that particular person.

Thus, the outplacement counseling specialist must be capable of recognizing how client responsibilities change as he moves from one consulting arena to another. This, of course, is a skill all management consultants (be they internal or external) must have as they work through the webs of relationships that must be sustained for effectiveness on any sensitive project.

What Constitutes an Outplacement Program?

A complete outplacement program includes a variety of services that meet the needs of both the company and the person being terminated. Depending on the particular circumstances of any one termination, some of these services may be more valuable than others. But the capacity to deliver each is characteristic of a true outplacement service.

Pretermination Consultation

Unfortunately, the outplacement specialist usually comes into the picture too late in the termination process. Ideally, he can offer advice long before the decision to terminate someone is final. In this role, the specialist can often help a manager think through the options or alternatives to termination and make sure the approach that is taken is objective and consistent with sound corporate policy.

In such a role the corporate outplacement counselor becomes an adviser to operating management in human resource problems. He becomes a resource management can use in reviewing its problems with poor performers. Plant or office personnel managers can also come to rely on the corporate OPC specialist as someone whose expertise is worth using as they deal with this most difficult area of personnel practice, which is on a par with recruiting, fair employment, affirmative action, compensation, and training and development.

All outplacement counselors have encountered cases in which, had things been handled differently, termination might have been avoided. To be effective, the OPC specialist must be viewed by managers as capable of providing valuable input on human resource development from a perspective broader than termination issues alone.

Whenever possible, the OPC specialist should work closely with the senior personnel officer in establishing corporate termination policy. Considerable direction in reviewing past termination practices to help form corporate procedures consistent with our discussion in Chapter 3 should also come from the OPC consultant.

Although ideal, involvement in such issues is not the norm. More typically, an OPC counselor finds himself about to enter a situation in which the events leading to the termination have not been well managed. In fact, the counselor is being asked to "pick up the pieces" that are expected to fall as a result of the termination. Management believes that supervision over the person being let go might have been more thorough, especially in the area of constructive criticism. It is hoped that the counselor can provide backup assistance in defusing what might be an exceptionally awkward or difficult firing.

Often, other characteristics complicate the issue: The subordinate is especially argumentative, is a member of a protected class under EEO legislation, or has considerable seniority with the company. Perhaps the manager doing the terminating simply has cold feet and needs some extra support.

What each of these situations has in common is that the OPC specialist doesn't become involved until it is too late to influence prior performance counseling with the subordinate or to monitor compliance with corporate policy. He is being placed on the firing line after most of the significant decisions have been made. His job at that point is to help management avoid or minimize the negative consequences of a less than ideal set of circumstances.

At that point the pretermination consultation is limited to a more specific set of factors:

1. Reviewing the support package and pointing out any areas that might have been overlooked (such as failure to specify references—a typical one).
2. Attaining agreement that the OPC counselor will approach management later with any request for adjustments in the support package that might prove important to the person being terminated (while cautioning management against agreeing to changes during the termination interview itself).
3. Reviewing the reasons the manager intends to give for firing the subordinate, making sure they are as descriptive and specific as possible.
4. Preparing the manager on how to conduct the interview.

In the pretermination consultation, the OPC specialist is trying to ensure that the person being terminated will be treated as professionally as possible by management and to help managers avoid falling into typical traps that will only complicate the process. Achieving these aims is a vital part of the OPC service.

Vocational and Career Path Consultation Resources

The person who has just been terminated has one overwhelming problem: to find another job. Right at the start of the job search process he has to settle several questions if he is to maximize his efforts. He has to define the type of job or jobs he is going to pursue. Which geographic location is he willing to accept? Indeed, if he is to take full advantage of a basically negative situation, he should examine his career carefully and perhaps redefine some of his career goals and job objectives. This is a good time for him to do a thorough self-assessment and to decide on any changes he wants to make.

The self-assessment may be the first thought he has ever given to the direction of his career. Outplacement counselors frequently encounter people who in college decided more or less to major in a given area, fell into their first jobs pretty much by chance, and began pursuing whatever career ladder those jobs seemed to afford them. Indeed, most career studies indicate that this is the typical pattern of career choice. An employee has often been drifting for some time before being terminated.

Today, there is a growing literature on career development, a literature that reflects our increasingly sophisticated understanding of the career process. The outplacement counselor should be capable of providing the terminated person with guidance in assessing his career.

Management-Style Consultation Resources

Often managers are terminated because their style of managing is so inflexible they encounter continual problems with subordinates, superiors, or others in the work environment. Failure to receive constructive feedback on this problem can lead to a pattern of job losses, with each job loss directly traceable to management style.

Outplacement counselors should be capable of addressing this issue. If the counselor's background is not good enough for him to provide substantive help in the area of manageral style, he should have access to others who are in a position to offer assistance.

At this point, the outplacement process is overlapping with aspects of management development work. There is reason to believe that a person's managerial style is not something that can easily be altered, especially in a short period of time. However, it is incumbent on the OPC counselor to make the manager aware of his problems in this area so that he can attempt to address his weaknesses in the years ahead. The counselor's work can do such things as:

Create awareness of the problem. Management-style inventories can be used to help the person identify how his style comes across to others. They are especially helpful if the data can be coupled with specific descriptive examples of the consequences of his approach in his previous job.

Focus on a few critical behaviors. Although the outplacement process is not designed to generate major changes in a person's behavior, it is often possible to identify one or two critical behaviors that, if toned down or altered, can make a difference in future job performance.

For example, one OPC client whom we'll call Jim was too rigid in his thinking. He always viewed issues in "either/or" terms, not dealing well with ambiguity. Once his mind was made up about some issue, he resisted the efforts of others to point out possible alternate courses of action. Since he tended to arrive at a decision early in a discussion, his subordinates saw him as arbitrary and close-minded. His superiors viewed him as impatient and argumentative. More to the point, his decisions often isolated his department from opportunities to be more effective. Ultimately, these personal characteristics cost him his job.

Initially, Jim resisted feedback from his counselor about his behavior, preferring to see himself as decisive rather than opinionated and rigid. Gradually, with the help of examples from his job search process, he came to accept that his decisiveness, when carried to an extreme, was getting him into difficulties. Working with his counselor, he agreed to a strategy in which once he had made up his mind he would assume that for some reason he was blocked from following that particular course of action. What would his backup strategy be? It wasn't easy, but gradually he came to train himself to look at another point of view. The end result was a less arbitrary approach to issues.

This is a good illustration of how counseling oriented to behavior change can help an outplacement counselee avoid repeating some of his past mistakes. When, for example, the source of the problem is a lack of training or experience, the counselor can direct a person toward learning opportunities.

Help the person understand the types of environments in which he is most likely to succeed or fail. Apart from attempting to alter certain pronounced aspects of a person's style, the outplacement process should result in his having a better self-understanding of his strengths and weaknesses. For example, if someone has a tendency to overcontrol people, while he strives to prevent this from becoming extreme, he can also work toward finding a job situation in which this characteristic is more likely to be a strength than a weakness. The situation might be one in which strong control over a disorganized department is required, for example.

Job Search Expertise

The heart of the outplacement counseling process is helping a person learn and execute the mechanics of an effective job search. This means that an OPC service needs extensive experience in résumé development and distribution planning and circulation of résumés, and expertise on how to be interviewed. The counselor should be the person to whom the job hunter can turn with questions on how to react to the many dilemmas that confront him in the process of looking for a position. The needs of the employee in this area are elaborated in Chapter 9. Working together the counselor and terminated employee can forge an individualized marketing strategy.

Secretarial Service

One of a person's biggest needs during a job search is secretarial support. There is a very real need for a manager to have access to someone who can type letters and résumés and take messages. Doing these things himself generally wastes valuable time, and often gives potential employers an impression of lack of organization. If the company has not otherwise arranged for such support, the outplacement service should be able to provide it.

Continuous Access for the Counselee Until Placement

The job search process consists of an ongoing series of stages. It is clear that a person can use support for more than the first few days after the termination. Of course, during the first few days he or she needs the most active and intensive support. A structured counseling program can provide someone with significant insights into both his past job performance and the nature of the problems that now confront him.

However, beyond this early learning process, the individual has a continuous need to be in touch with his counselor in order to ask questions that relate to his marketing strategy or the process of finalizing a job. Indeed, the lack of someone to talk to who is knowledgeable about these kinds of issues is often a major problem confronting an unemployed person.

This being the case, the extent to which a person can have periodic conversations with his counselor determines the extent of the helpfulness of the outplacement support. Therefore, although the terminated person is certainly going to need less extensive help from the counselor once he or she begins actively to look for work, any program that allows for continued availability of the counselor is going to be of more benefit to the person receiving the service. This type of continuing support is most easily provided by external consultants.

Continuous Feedback to Management Until Placement

Even though the terminated person is no longer an employee, most managers find themselves wondering what progress he or she is making toward finding a job. Having gone through the effort of arranging for outplacement counseling support, it is reasonable for management to expect to be informed of the person's status. This has the obvious advantages of satisfying the organization's need to know what has been purchased with its investment in outplacement counseling and of providing some support for the conscience of the manager who did the firing.

There is also the need to demonstrate interest and support to other employees. Once the terminated person finds a new position, he is often appreciative of how his old employer didn't simply dump him without any continuing concern. This sentiment has a way of getting back to former associates who are still employed in the organization.

Furthermore, management is then in a position to be knowledgeable about the ex-employee's status. When someone asks "How is Bill making out?" and the manager who did the firing answers "I have no idea," his subordinates are being given concrete evidence of why they shouldn't be too concerned about loyalty to the company.

Pretermination consultation, vocational guidance services, managerial-style counseling services, job search expertise, secretarial services, continuous access to the counselor, and continuous feedback to management up to the time of placement—these are the elements a full, complete outplacement support program should have the potential of delivering. Of course, like any other part of the support package, the extent of the benefits provided will reflect on the level of the employee being severed. However, any full and complete outplacement program includes the ability to deliver each of these services.

The problems that confront the terminated person in looking for another job are complex and, in some cases, are likely to stretch out the period of unemployment. The process is complicated by the fact that being terminated often arouses strong emotions regarding failure on the job and how to relate to friends, family, and other people whose esteem they value. Through providing a structured outplacement service, the company can go a long way toward repaying an employee for efforts made in the past at least to try to do a good job by alleviating some of the problems brought on by the loss of his or her job. In so doing, a company extends its sense of obligation to its employees and protects itself with those people who remain behind.

8

Counseling the Terminated Executive

FOR THE AVERAGE EXECUTIVE, BEING UNEM-
ployed and seeking work is a rare experience. Many
managers never encounter the problem; others face it only
a couple of times throughout their careers. Being recruited to
another company does not count, nor does soliciting job opportunities while solidly employed. The problems and pressures confronting the terminated executive are more extensive, more in-
tense, and generally just different from those experienced in
either of the other two situations.

Therefore, it is reasonable to expect a manager to be naive
about the details of conducting a job search when he or she has
been terminated. The problem has probably never come up before; if it did, it wasn't recently.

On the other hand, corporations are regularly besieged by
managers looking for work. They hire people on a regular basis.
Typically, formal systems are in place that give the companies an
aura of sophistication and competency often markedly lacking in
the approach of the applicant. This contrast is intensified by the

fact that the terminated executive is more anxious about being hired than the corporation is about making an employment decision. Thus, even the most experienced managers many times appear naive and amateurish as they enter the job market.

Problems apart from the job search process can exacerbate the situation. If there have been problems at work, these difficulties can have an unsettling effect on other areas of an executive's life. Poor work performance can, of course, be the result of domestic troubles. Either way, problems on the job are often interwoven with difficulties in a person's personal life.

The terminated executive is often in a state of shock. As asserted in previous chapters, the manager may or may not receive emotional support from family members. In either case the situation is awkward for all concerned as the manager tries to protect a damaged ego. Typically, questions of self-worth are seldom far from his or her mind.

If the termination was not well handled, the manager is probably confused about what went wrong on the job. Anger, resentment, or bitterness can emerge and find expression in counterproductive ways. In short, the need for counseling is real and it goes beyond the typical "how to find a job" variety.

The above points can be illustrated by two cases from our files. First let's look at the story of Harry Chandler.

Harry was a general foreman in a large production facility who had been left on the job for more than 15 years with very little training. There was a change in management and Harry was discharged. In typical fashion, he was fired on a Friday afternoon.

When he arrived at the counselor's office on Monday at 10:00 A.M., Harry was noticeably shaken; in fact, he was physically shaking and he stammered throughout the interview. For two hours he went on over and over again about how the company was his life and how he never thought he would be terminated. He continually stated he would never get another job.

As so often happens, we had no opportunity to counsel with the firm prior to the termination. It contacted us on the day before the firing, with the process already set in motion. As near as we could determine, the new management felt Harry represented an old philosophy, a philosophy that was keeping the company from growing. In essence, Harry was a symbolic firing. Getting rid of him meant getting rid of "old" attitudes.

The termination had completely destroyed Harry's confidence. Coming from a situation that provided little training or development, he was convinced he would be uncompetitive in the job market. Even if he were hired, Harry felt he would be unable to make the grade. That was how he interpreted his being singled out for "housecleaning" by the new management.

In truth, Harry was not the most attractive job candidate. But he had 15 years of experience. What he needed was help in targeting his job opportunities and willingness to sell himself. First, he had to see that he had something to sell.

It took 30 hours of counseling before Harry felt prepared to face a job interview. During this counseling, Harry came to understand that in a production situation he had many strengths. He was strong technically, he could deal with other supervisors effectively, and he had a strong record in cost control. He was also capable of learning new techniques and functioning in a different environment.

After eight months, Harry found a job both he and his counselor felt he could handle. During those eight months he received 63 hours of personal counseling. This substantial effort proved to be the deciding factor in rebuilding his confidence to the point where he could go out and find a job. Harry's feedback to us was that the counseling was the one thing that helped him hold his life together during this crisis. Four years later, he is still employed and happy with his job.

The story of John Rodin is somewhat different. John was a high-level executive with an Ivy League background. He was terminated from his job after a decline in his job performance over a period of three years. With the pretermination counseling of Drake Beam Morin, he was terminated on a Thursday afternoon and met with the outplacement counselor right after his termination. The next day John started his formal OPC program.

During the first week of counseling John began to discuss how there had been increasing stress in his home life over the past few years. He felt his family situation was deteriorating. His unemployment was placing still more strain on the relatonship with his wife. There was an element of desperation in his comments. Having lost his job, he feared his marriage was coming apart as well.

As we do in the normal course of counseling, we invited the spouse to visit our offices and spend time with our psychologist and the counselor working with her husband. Discussions with the spouse uncovered a lot of hostility on her part, much of it centered around feelings of exclusion from her husband's working life. His career was consuming him and she felt she was not sharing life with him. There was reason to believe that the undercurrent of stress at home was contributing to John's problems on the job. He was aware of the tension but didn't understand it or know how to deal with it.

In this instance, the counseling provided was directed toward both he spouse and the executive. In addition to helping the executive in his job search, the couple examined their marriage and how they used their time together. Their relationship was reestablished and the executive obtained a new position, with an increase in compensation.

In both cases, the terminated person had to overcome obstacles other than the immediately obvious one of finding new employment. Harry lacked the confidence even to begin looking for a job. His previous work situation, coupled with the mishandling of the termination, had destroyed something very basic—his sense of competence. All the years of working in supervision without the benefit of opportunities for development had created in Harry a dependency on the company. Suddenly cut loose, without warning and as a symbol of "what is wrong around here," Harry had no concept of what else he could do.

John, on the other hand, was fighting a battle on two fronts.

His career was coming apart and his marriage was floundering. He had little insight into what was wrong in either case. Each was a distraction from the other. John had made all the right moves and had succeeded only at mucking things up.

Clearly Harry was in no position to be effective in job interviews. John's position wasn't much better. He had to sell himself, yet unlike the last time he went after a job, he had real doubts about his ability to deliver.

The Role of the Outplacement Counselor

What are the implications for the counselor? From both of the above cases, we can see that outplacement counseling is typically more complex than other variations of job search coaching. The termination process can intensify and bring to the surface problems that hinder the person's ability to find as well as keep a job. But the counselor should resist any tendency to play the role of lay psychologist. He or she should avoid becoming involved in problems that go beyond his or her expertise. In the emotionally charged atmosphere of a termination, it is as easy to do harm as good.

What is needed is a delicate balance between the sensitivity to perceive the various pressures that come to bear on the terminated executive and a willingness to recognize when these pressures are best handled by another professional. Throughout the process the counselor needs perseverance in providing support and direction to the client, even when the job search process seems stalled.

For example, one man—we'll call him Mike—was, at the age of 61, described as "Peter principled" or "plateaued" out by his boss, who had only recently terminated him. After the termination was completed the company decided to provide outplacement counseling, in deference to Mike's 33 years with the company. Holding the title of director, finance department, at the time of his termination, Mike vowed not to accept retirement.

The counseling process with Mike continued over two years, during which the counselor and Mike met periodically. During these meetings the counselor made suggestions for using what was becoming a wide network of contacts and discussed methods for turning an obvious disadvantage—age—into a strength. Perhaps more importantly, the counselor helped Mike clarify his reasons for not retiring and the type of company that might be most interested in his services. For much of the two years the counselor was a source of moral support, someone who would catch Mike up when his search efforts began to get sloppy out of frustration.

At the age of 63, Mike obtained a job as manager of internal control in a small company that needed his expertise. Three years later, Mike is flourishing, along with his new company. Except for the age factor, which complicated his situation by realistically eliminating many employment opportunities, Mike's case typifies one in which the outplacement counselor plays a meaningful role. The counselor did what he was supposed to do by recognizing the motivations and needs of the terminated person and providing meaningful direction within the framework of these needs. The counselor recognized the importance of Mike's need to remain in private industry; it was what Mike knew and how he defined himself. At the same time, the counselor gave Mike realistic advice on the possibilities open to him.

Harry's case afforded the same challenge to the counselor. Harry needed concrete help in coming to define himself correctly in the job market. He also needed the skills and perseverance to market himself correctly.

In the case of John, however, the outplacement counselor perceived problems apart from the workplace. He therefore recommended that John and his wife consult a psychologist who was trained to deal with the issues involved. Effective outplacement counselors must be prepared to refer people to psychologists or psychiatrists when problems outside of their competency emerge.

The role of the outplacement counselor is one to which it is not always easy to adhere. Once a relationship of trust is established it is easy for a counselor to delve into areas in which he or she has little or no training. At the other extreme, a counselor can be so intent at fitting a client into a "packaged" job search process that important issues are ignored. Clearly, the middle ground is marked by ambiguity. In each case the professional outplacement counselor strives to adjust to the situation at hand, always mindful of the need for using other professional resources.

A Model for Outplacement Counseling

Establishment of an effective counseling relationship does not happen by chance. The successful counselor works hard at it. As in any area of sensitive interpersonal communication, it is helpful for the counselor to have a model that can assist in structuring his or her relationship with the client. The model offered below summarizes the steps our counselors go through during the course of an OPC relationship.

Step 1. Introduction
Step 2. Diffusing Feelings
Step 3. Contracting
Step 4. Job Search Counseling
  • Getting organized
  • Developing a personal marketing game plan
  • Selling one's abilities
Step 5. Monitoring

Step 1. Introduction

In practice an outplacement counselor can find himself or herself meeting the client under any one of a number of circumstances. However, in terms of frequency of occurrence, two prevail. First, and preferred, the terminated executive meets the counselor immediately after the termination interview. This is best done by having the counselor waiting in a conference room or a private office on the company's premises, but removed from the immediate work area of the person being discharged. The person can then be introduced to the counselor right after the termination interview.

This permits the counselor to deal with the person's initial reaction to the termination. It is especially helpful for the counselor to be in a position to advise the terminated manager on his immediate activities. Unfortunately, many managers who have just been terminated panic and begin calling their friends and industry contacts. At this point the person is seldom in a position to use these contacts wisely. Thus, all he or she accomplishes is to alert contacts to his or her distress. The terminated person uses up these valuable resources without getting anything in return.

Frequently the terminated person is concerned about what to tell friends and family. This can prolong an initial reaction of disbelief. Having the counselor meet with the person right after the termination interview places him or her in a position to serve as a resource when many managers truly need assistance.

The other place for the initial meeting is at the counselor's office after the termination, usually a day later. This arrangement obviously makes it impossible for the counselor to help the person during the first 12 to 24 hours after the firing.

In any event, during the initial introduction the counselor should be sure to cover these points:

- The types of services that will be provided.
- The limitations on these services.
- The nature of the counselor–client relationship.

In describing the services that will be provided the counselor wants to give an overview, not a detailed explanation of the entire counseling process. This is especially true when meeting the person right after the termination interview has been completed. Typically, the person is too distressed and distracted to remember details. What the counselor wants to do is impress on the person that a structured process exists that will help him or her to take constructive action in dealing with the present predicament. We usually do this by outlining the major steps of the process and impressing on the person that he or she has a place to go during the next workday.

In describing the outplacement services, the counselor should state that he or she will be there to advise the person during the job search process, not to find the person employment. This is the principal limitation to OPC services. The discharged employee should never be given the impression that it is the counselor's job to find him or her employment or make critical career decisions.

This point can be made gently: "You now have a new job—finding another position. The process I have been describing can help you do that, but you'll find it necessary to make some important decisions. My job is to work with you and share our experience with you as you go about the task of seeking employment." This kind of statement helps structure the relationship between client and counselor in a healthy fashion.

Equally important is avoiding statements that promise assistance the counselor cannot deliver. For example, one counselor had a tendency to refer people to a certain person in an executive search firm. The implication was that this person's contacts would lead to employment. After six or so referrals the contact in the search firm requested that his name not be used any more. In addition, not one of the people sent to the firm ever got a job through the contact. Hence, the counselor ended up irritating both the search organization and the people sent there for counsel. Most counselors learn early that they should not make statements about providing help when they cannot make good on them.

Finally the counselor should state clearly that although the expense of the OPC service is being borne by the former employer, the counselor's client is the terminated employee. The distinction between sponsor (the ex-employer) and client (the discharged person) should be emphasized. Any questions the person may have should be answered directly and honestly. These questions typically relate to the services themselves, the counselor's role in the termination, and/or how long the person might be unemployed. All answers should be straightforward. However, the counselor should call attention to the person's severance benefits, which mean he or she has some breathing room. It is important that the time be used effectively.

One person we worked with stated that he was going to postpone looking for a job until he had used up a good portion of his severance pay. The counselor responded by pointing out that no one could force him to look for a job. However, the exact length of time required to locate a position was unpredictable. By adopting such an approach the person was running the risk of hurting himself. The counselor suggested he first examine the job search process before making up his mind on timing.

Of course, the counselor recognized that the person's statement had been motivated by vindictiveness and a sense of powerlessness. The next steps enabled him to get these feelings off his chest. Having done so, he began his job search immediately.

Step 2. Diffusing Feelings

Generally, the introductory step is brief—fifteen minutes or so. Its basic purpose is to take the first step in structuring the counselor–client relationship. The next step can be a crucial one—helping the person express his or her feelings about having been terminated. Sometimes this is an easy step to initiate. The person is disturbed and wants to ventilate his or her feelings. This is especially true if the person's reaction is one of disbelief or violent shock.

Other times the person may not express his or her feelings right away, particularly if the reaction is anticipatory, euphoric, or escapist. In these cases the terminated manager may adopt a posture of nonconcern or minimize his or her reaction. The counselor needs to probe and get the person to open up.

In pursuing this step the counselor has two objectives. The first is to give the person an opportunity to ventilate and get issues that can serve as a distraction off his or her chest. If these problems remain buried beneath the surface of the person's conversation they can not only impede preparation for the job search, but also surface at an inappropriate time.

In one instance a terminated manager felt considerable resentment toward his former employer. However, his initial position was that "Things were not handled well and I got the short end of the stick, but that's over now and it's not worth talking about." Later, he let his anger come out at a social gathering within hearing distance of some influential people in his area of expertise. He came across as bitter and succeeded in minimizing their willingness to refer him to contacts.

The counselor's second objective during this step is to listen carefully and attempt to identify what concerns on the part of the person may be intensifying his or her reaction. As we saw earlier in this chapter with Harry, sometimes the person is afraid that he or she is not trained well enough to be marketable. Family concerns or fears about age might be underlying his or her reaction. Some people are concerned about saving face with colleagues or friends. Any of these fears can prolong a person's initial reaction.

Thus, while the terminated manager is ventilating, the counselor can be getting clues as to the person's true concerns. These concerns are critical to the success of the outplacement counseling process. Typically, the counselor can begin this step of the process with a broad, open-ended remark: "Tell me how you feel about the way in which the termination was handled." "How do you feel about the way you've been treated?"

The counselor should stay in a listening mode, using the same listening skills discussed in Chapter 6—open-ended questions, restatement, expanders, and silence. If the person initially avoids talking about his or her feelings, the counselor should attempt to overcome this avoidance syndrome with additional questions. For example:

Counselor   At this point, what are your feelings toward your old employer?

Client   Obviously, not good. But it doesn't do any good worrying about it, does it?

Counselor   Sometimes a good place to begin is examining what went wrong. What events led up to your termination?

Client   Events! Hell, the guy was impossible to work for! He never gives any meaningful direction to his people.

Counselor   You feel he wasn't supportive.

Client   It was more than lack of support. Take the time. . . .

As you can see, once the client got talking, there was plenty of hostility expressed, hostility that needed to be discussed.

Sometimes a terminated person is so emotional that Steps 1 and 2 must be reversed. Considerable diffusing of feelings must precede even the introduction to the outplacement services. In one case the terminated manager came into the office to meet the counselor in an agitated state. His opening comment was: "How can they do this? No warning! I was doing my job just like everyone else. Well, they aren't going to get away with this!"

He proceeded to talk for half an hour about how unfair his boss was and how he was going to demand an explanation from senior management. After he had quieted down the counselor explained that senior management was aware of the termination and although he could request an audience with someone at a higher level it was not going to change anything. The counselor advised the man to treat his current status as a given and went on to introduce the kind of help that was being offered through OPC.

At this point the two began exploring the events that preceded the termination in order to facilitate a further diffusion of feelings.

Step 3. Contracting

Once feelings have been aired it is possible for the counselor to establish a psychological contract between himself or herself and the terminated person. This may happen as part of the initial conversation; more often it occurs during the second meeting.

Contracting involves a clarification of expectations on the part of both parties. This process can be initiated by the counselor providing a more detailed description of the outplacement process and emphasizing the nature of his or her role. It includes reiteration of the fact that the counselor can assist the terminated executive in developing his job search skills, but can't get him a job. In fact, the counselor's expectation is that the terminated executive will approach the job search process as his current job.

The counselor also needs to ask how the process meets the person's expectations. It is especially important that the two discuss the allocation of the counselor's time and the amount of access the client will have to the counselor.

Usually, OPC is loaded at the front end, in the sense that a counselor works intensely with a terminated person during the first week or so after the termination. The counselor devotes this time to getting the terminated person to follow a structured program designed to prepare him or her for the job search process. After this activity the client assumes increasing responsibility for the job search, with the counselor providing periodic advice and support.

It is critical that the client understand how the process works. Earlier we spoke of the need for the counselor to avoid creating a sense of dependency on himself. Sometimes the client will strive to create the dependency and end up using the counselor as a crutch. If and when this type of behavior emerges, having explicitly discussed expectations makes it easier for the counselor to confront the client with the behavior.

The counselor should also inform the client that periodically he will report his progress in finding a job to his former employer. These brief status reports are only to inform the sponsor that the counselor is continuing to work with the client and will not reveal any confidential information. If the terminated person learns about these status reports during the job search process and was formerly unaware they were being submitted, he or she may feel the counselor is manipulating the relationship.

Step 4. Job Search Counseling

Job search counseling is the heart of the outplacement counseling process. Obviously, the counselor needs a thorough understanding of the job search process. His advice in this area will be critical to the terminated employee. The counselor must be especially sensitive to the pressures of the job search process as they are experienced by someone who is unemployed and coming off a less than successful work experience.

For the purpose of discussion, the many problems that confront the manager can be put under three general headings:

Getting organized
Developing a personal marketing game plan
Selling one's abilities

Let's consider each in turn.

Getting Organized

The worst mistake a terminated manager can make is to think of himself as entering an idle period. In reality, he now has a job; namely, to package and market himself. If he is to be successful, he must approach this job with the same vigor, imagination, and discipline that would categorize his approach to any other important task.

Becoming impatient and expecting overnight success is the pitfall of many a job search. Most positions at the managerial level are not advertised publicly. Some have not even crystallized within the company, but are triggered by the arrival of the applicant. Outplacement consultants refer to this as the hidden job market. Prematurely jumping into job interviews and exhausting contacts with colleagues tends to work against the applicant since he is seldom in a position to look for and recognize potential opportunities. Surfacing good job situations requires discipline and a systematic approach.

This advice is more easily given than practiced. The trauma associated with the interruption of employment naturally generates strong feelings. These may include shock, disbelief, anger, grief, anxiety, depression, self-doubt, humiliation, shame, fear—a whole gamut of negative feelings. People experience different mixtures of these feelings at different times after a dismissal. Their feelings tend to change or even recur as they progress with their job search. However, to give way to such feelings for an extended period is no more productive than it would be in any job situation.

More specifically, these feelings can lead to prolonged periods of spinning one's wheels while feeling sorry for oneself. Bitterness can noticeably enter a person's conversation. Some people succumb to the temptation to take a breather for a while and go on a vacation. Still others embark immediately on an almost manic period of activity, contacting everyone they know in their industry, sending out résumés in an effort to demonstrate they are not taking this lying down. Any of the above reactions is self-defeating. Now more than ever, the manager needs to plan his activity thoroughly. It is the counselor's job to help diffuse the counterproductive impulses and help the person plan and structure his or her time wisely.

Relationships with the Former Company

One area a terminated manager must get firmly under control is his relationship with his former company. Although the employment relationship is being severed, the former company is in a position to be of assistance to the discharged manager. Furthermore, since executive circles in many industries and/or functional specialties are relatively small, the terminated manager is likely to continue to encounter many former colleagues.

For obvious reasons these relationships can be delicate. The company is often relieved to have the person gone and wants to put the whole matter in the past. The terminated person can be both embarrassed and angry during encounters with former associates. As in a divorce, simple inquiries can be perceived as unreasonable demands and statements of corporate policy can seem like justification for abandonment.

Judy Gentry was typical in this regard. She was not sure just what kind of a recommendation she would get from her former boss. Her suspicion was that he was never comfortable with a woman in her former job, and she could not see him going out of his way for her. When she encountered former associates she had a tendency to refer to her ex-boss as "an amateur who was easily threatened." Her former associates said little. Her boss was simply glad everything was over.

In an atmosphere such as this, an outplacement counselor has a vital role to play. The first step is to sit down with the person and review the support package and determine what, if any, conditions should be clarified with the former employer. The counselor can be an intermediary in this process.

In Judy's case the counselor talked to her former boss and obtained agreement on the "official story" on why Judy was dismissed. He was able to tell her what kind of recommendation she would get. At the same time, the counselor got Judy to see that, no matter what her assessment of her boss, her comments were coming across as sour grapes. Few of her associates were likely to introduce her to potential employment contacts when her manner was so bitter.

No matter how the person may feel, it is profitable for him or her to remain outwardly calm and cool. If, perchance, he or she has the need to go further into the reasons for being terminated with the ex-boss, it is often wise to postpone this until he or she has calmed down. Nothing is to be gained by indulging in any recriminations with a former boss, the personnel department, or anyone else that may have been involved in the termination process.

An important part of the counselor's role is to help the ex-employee to recognize this fact. Often the first step is for the counselor to hear out the person's complaints (Step 2 of the model), providing an opportunity for him to air his feelings of frustration in a safe environment. Once this has been done, if the person feels something can be learned from an objective review of his performance, the counselor can try to set up such a discussion with the counselor present. More typically, the counselor and the terminated manager assess what happened from the information already at hand.

The behavior of the person toward his former business associates can either enhance or prove to be a drag on his job search efforts. Either way it is clear that once again the person is faced with a series of awkward and complex decisions regarding how he should act toward people he is accustomed to seeing and may still see on a regular basis. Lack of previous experience in this kind of situation can create unnecessary stress and strain on valuable relationships with others if the individual does not receive proper and experienced advice.

Dealings with People Away from the Workplace

On the home front, some executives try to keep their dismissal a secret from their wives and children. Although this has to be a personal decision, it is our experience that it is best to share the situation with family members in a mature way, involving them in the current crisis.

Spouses many times find themselves unsure of how to react. If they act indifferent, it appears that they are abandoning their partner in a time of crisis. If they act supportive, their partner sometimes becomes even more defensive and resistant. All too easily the spouse's position can deteriorate into a "can't win" situation. Holding on to a mature relationship under these stressful conditions is no easy task.

The family's task can be lightened, however, if the counselor is able to get the discharged manager to understand the dilemmas that confront family members. Tensions will exist, but the executive can learn to step back and help defuse them. Part and parcel of this mature approach is the person's coming to understand that termination is a temporary setback, not a sign of total failure.

Of course, many times the family is something less than supportive. In our experience, close to half the executives who have been discharged confront a response on the home front of "Well, what did you do wrong this time?" Hostility is directed toward the individual and blame is placed on his shoulders for this new and very real threat to the security of the family. This attitude, of course, places an even greater strain on him. In any event, family involvement is an issue that needs to be handled delicately.

For this reason we invite the spouse to meet with the counselor as part of the OPC process. Frequently, both partners will express feelings of underlying tension in their relationship after the termination. The counselor can help them to talk to each other about these feelings and agree on a posture with which each can be comfortable. It is important that the couple comes to realize that these pressures are typical and will ease once the terminated person resettles into another job.

Of even more importance, the couple is jointly making career and life-style decisions. If the tensions that arise after the termination are allowed to sever communication between husband and wife, job decisions may be made that create a future strain on the relationship. For this reason it is imperative that the counselor strive to get both partners to understand that having been fired doesn't represent permanent failure; it happens to many successful people.

As we saw earlier in this chapter, sometimes the counseling process reveals personal difficulties that require specialized, professional help. John Rodin was fortunate that his counselor was competent enough to be supportive of such professional assistance.

As for contacts with the outside world, things need to be kept as normal as possible. The worst thing someone can do is withdraw into a shell. If the matter of his job change comes up in conversations with neighbors and friends, it should be discussed factually, using the same approach that will be used with potential employers and avoiding any bitterness or criticism of the former company or associates. These stories somehow seem to get back to the person discussed with an amazing degree of frequency and can only serve to hurt the terminated person.

At times the counselor can help prepare both the terminated person and the spouse by role playing with them, acting out how they are going to deal with social and professional contacts. Once a person hears himself or herself explain what has happened and comes to understand some of the emotions felt while talking about it, the couple is better prepared to deal with the outside world. In fact, once the two of them overcome any sense of humiliation, the discharged person can start to involve contacts in his or her job search.

Career Planning

As early as possible after the termination, the ex-employee needs to begin thinking about his or her career and start making decisions that are ultimately going to influence the marketing strategy. First, career goals need to be assessed thoroughly. There is a growing research literature that indicates that everybody passes through career stages.

Often the goals that were attractive to somebody early in his or her work career are less attractive once he or she reaches mid-life or a more advanced age. Certain career goals may already have been reached, while others may realistically be unattainable. Thought about one's career objectives is fundamental before anyone starts to consider the kinds of jobs and labor markets in which to concentrate job search efforts.

In one recent case a middle-level executive came to realize that making it to a high-level position was not really important to him any more. He wanted to live comfortably and enjoy his family. He also did not want to relocate. Having transferred three times during his career, he was beginning to put down roots and develop a sense of being part of a community.

Even more importantly, he came to realize that part of his problem in his old job was that he was working at cross purposes with some of the younger people who were moving up around him. He resented their progress, yet his heart was not in making significant sacrifices to continue advancing his own career. The result was a destructive resistance toward his associates. With a clearer understanding of his career objectives, he would not make the same mistake again.

Part of the career planning process should include a thorough self-assessment. Not only should a person look at his career goals and job objectives but he should also do a careful analysis of past strengths and weaknesses in performing the job. What things does he do really well? What special skills have elicited compliments or have successfully helped advance his career? What, realistically, are that person's weaknesses? One advantage the experienced executive has over the recent graduate in approaching the job market is that the older, more experienced person has more data on his or her abilities and can have a more realistic picture of the type of job at which he or she is likely to be successful.

Along with the question of what one can do well is the issue of what one really wants to do. Counselors often have the client assess his or her job history. Of all the various assignments with which the person has been involved, which ones were truly interesting and satisfying?

In our experience, many people come to the realization that they haven't been happy for the past six or seven years simply because their job situation was not one in which they were particularly interested, nor was it leading to relevant career goals. In this sense the client comes to realize that perhaps termination was not a wholly bad thing.

Developing a Personal Marketing Game Plan

Once the person has completed the basic step of getting organized, it is time to begin evolving a marketing strategy. Just as the success of any business enterprise rests on its ability to market its product or services successfully, so, too, does the success of a person's job search depend on his or her approach to marketing the talents being offered to prospective employers.

No major corporation would leave its marketing strategy to amateurs. Indeed, companies employ the best talent they can find in order to make sure all the key pieces of an effective marketing strategy are in place. However, most people approaching the job market are amateurs at marketing themselves. The simple fact is they have never had to confront the problem of marketing themselves before.

But just as there are proven skills in corporate marketing, there are established methods that are known to be effective in marketing oneself for a job. One of the greatest needs a person has when entering the job market is access to those kinds of skills—learning one way or another how to make a product of their career planning efforts and convert it into an effective personal marketing game plan.

Some of the elements of a successful marketing strategy are well known to managers. Others are easily overlooked. However, well known or not, the ability to adapt these elements to one's own particular situation and make intelligent choices among the available options requires a certain degree of sophistication.

Helping the client develop a marketing game plan starts with a systematic review of the basic elements common to all successful job searches:

- Constructing a résumé
- Developing a contact network
- Contacting target companies

All three are illustrated in the marketing game plan of Peter Hill.

PETER HILL

Peter Hill was a 44-year-old executive with an extensive background in sales, market research, and finance. Virtually his entire career had been spent with three manufacturing firms. This was the first time he had been discharged from a job.

Like many people, Peter got started in the manufacturing sector because of a good job offer when he left school. Thus, he had fallen into his career. Despite his industrial background, for some time now he had harbored a personal dream of going into retailing. Eventually he wanted to own his own store. However, he had no real experience in this area.

In thinking about his career objectives both he and his wife decided it was now or never if he hoped to own his own business. The first step was to try to get a position with a large retail organization in order to learn the business and make contacts. Recognizing that the switch would be difficult, Peter and his wife resolved to do it anyway.

Preparing a Résumé

The chronological résumé, which lists one's various jobs in reverse order with the most recent first, is the most common.

Since that is what most employers expect to see and are comfortable reviewing, the majority of executives seeking work are best served by using that particular format.

However, Peter's counselor suggested a functional résumé, which avoids or plays down the employment record. Instead, it features a summary of the kinds of functions in which the person has worked. Since Pete was seeking to change his career path radically, he and his counselor felt he would be better off with a functional résumé. It would allow him to emphasize skills and expertise and divert the interviewer's attention from the fact that he was attempting to enter a different type of industry—retailing. Unfortunately, many prospective employers fail to interview a job applicant simply because the chronological résumé indicates the applicant has spent most of his or her career in a sector of the economy foreign to their particular organization.

Through conversations with friends and acquaintances working in large retail companies, Pete learned which critical skills were sought after and the type of position for which he would be best suited. His initial goal was to "crack" the industry. Having done his homework, Peter constructed a functional résumé that highlighted his marketing and cost control skills.

Developing a Contact Network

Contacts are a person's most important job-seeking resource, provided he or she develops and uses them correctly. We have discovered that the majority of the people we work with find their jobs through personal contacts.

Since Pete was attempting to change industries, he felt he could not rely heavily on his personal contacts, since most of his sources were not in retailing. Still, at his counselor's urging, he pumped some of his former associates for introductions to friends in retailing. Ask most people for suggestions about people who would be possible sources of job opportunities and they will draw a blank. However, systematically interviewing people, running down possibilities, and suggesting some possible areas in which the job seeker is interested—these are all ways of stimulating creativity on the part of the people who make up one's contact network.

Pete was surprised by the number of leads he got from former associates. By asking them about people in specific companies, he got his former colleagues to recall neighbors, school buddies, or members of professional societies who were in retailing. For example, his former industrial relations manager knew the vice-president of personnel at two large retailers from professional personnel society meetings.

Soon he had evolved a list of specific people—from friends, associates, and industry publications—who could help him in his job search. Initially, he contacted people to whom he had the advantage of a personal introduction. His counselor advised him to approach these people on the basis of learning more about the industry and not of finding a job in their organization. This way he found it easier to get an appointment. Soon he was evolving an extensive set of contacts and had elicited a few hints of interest.

Contacting Target Companies

As his job search became more focused, he began contacting companies he knew had a need for someone with his skills. His counselor helped him with his cover letters and taught him how to get past a secretary on the phone in order to set up a personal appointment.

He avoided wasting time contacting search firms and answering newspaper ads. The larger search firms receive hundreds of résumés per day and, naturally, these have to be screened by a low-level staff person at a high rate of speed. A fair-sized space ad in *The New York Times* for a position that is at all attractive commonly draws 500 to 1,000 replies. Therefore, unless a person has outstanding qualifications and is a perfect fit for a given job, merely mailing a résumé to a search firm or to an ad placer is ineffective. Given the nature of Pete's experience, his counselor advised him against investing his time in these pursuits.

In short, Pete had to tailor his marketing strategy to his particular situation. Four and a half months after he had been terminated he found a job in retailing—one he felt would provide the exposure he wanted.

Selling One's Abilities

Once the marketing strategy works and the person is invited for an interview, the real selling takes place. As any salesperson can tell you, a good firm lead is helpful, but it doesn't make the sale. All that résumés, cover letters, and contact networks can do is get the person a meaningful appointment. Then the real work begins.

Personnel consultants are well aware that there is a considerable demand for seminars in *how to be interviewed.* It reflects a growing awareness that how one handles oneself during the employment interview is a critical factor in landing a good job.

In fact, in the first few seconds of an interview, perhaps while the person is still getting himself seated, he will convey some important impressions that often lead the interviewer subconsciously to reach a conclusion. Proper dress, getting rid of outer clothing such as coat and overshoes before coming into the interviewer's office, and meeting the person with a firm handshake accompanied by a smile are important aspects of the interview process. They help project an image, and that image will work either for the person being interviewed or against him.

Once the interview begins, it is important to be in a position to handle questions effectively. Prior to arriving at the interview, the interviewee should have given some thought to handling difficult questions, questions such as "What is motivating you to change jobs?" "Why did your previous company let you go?" "If I were to contact your former boss, what would he be likely to tell me about you?" "What are your major weaknesses?" These questions need to be answered smoothly and believably.

For example, Pete needed to be able to give convincing answers on why he wished to make a switch over to retailing. Pete talked about the flair of retailing, which he liked, and the fact that he felt his previous experience provided him with skills useful in a low-margin business. He felt his unique background would provide opportunities for advancement once he adjusted to the retailing environment. He also learned to express concisely how he had adapted rapidly to new work environments in the past. Pete and his counselor role-played interviews on video tape over and over again. From friends in retailing he picked up key words and behaviors that would help him sell himself to an employer.

Equally important is a person's ability to answer the most positive questions. The person should be able to give an overview of his professional life. This should be brief and concise. It should be a capsule-size briefing that takes from one and a half to two minutes. Beyond that the person should have memorized four to six of his primary accomplishments and feed these into the interview so that they flow into the conversation. All of this, of course, requires thorough preparation before arriving at the interview. It is especially helpful if the person has been able to rehearse the interview and receive professional feedback on how he is coming across.

Step 5. Monitoring

Once the executive is actively involved in the job search process, the counselor's role becomes one of periodic review and supportive advice. For example, it is important that the job hunter recognize when a job opportunity is getting serious. Otherwise, he or she may suddenly be called upon to enter into final negotiations or even be pressed for a decision without being fully prepared.

Many job candidates need help in how to approach a potential employer with whom they have had several interviews but with whom they are still not sure where they stand. It is both a pleasant and agonizing experience to have more than one job offer either in hand or apparently close. When a job hunter has three or four offers pending, it almost always seems that the company he favors has not made a firm offer while another is pressing him hard for a decision on its offer.

There are many reasons companies may be seriously interested in a candidate but have not gotten around to making an offer. Often, hiring someone at the middle to upper level requires groups of people to meet and approve the appointment—the salary committee, the board, the executive committee. Perhaps one of the key people has been traveling or pressing business matters have made it impossible for the necessary people to get together and consider the person's candidacy.

In such a case, if the company pressing him is a viable opportunity in his eyes, the person is obligated to lean gently on the lagging companies, saying something like "In order to deal forthrightly with this other company, I feel obligated to give it an answer on its fine offer, but I would really prefer to hear something from you, and I am hoping it will be attractive too." The counselor should help prepare the person to deal with such issues as they arise.

Sometimes an important part of the monitoring step is simply helping the person to keep up his or her morale and keep the job search process in perspective. Just as some terminated people are fearful about their ability to find work, others are overly optimistic. For such people, the realities of looking for a job come as a shock.

In any case, the sense of isolation people frequently experience when they find themselves terminated can be overwhelming. As they go about preparing for the job search, questions keep popping into their minds. Decisions are repeatedly made without any opportunity to assess which course of action might be the most effective way of proceeding.

A person's family frequently has little or no experience on which to draw in attempting to help him. Friends can offer conflicting advice, much of which is not reliable or comes from people who have no more experience in this area than the person who is out on the job market. Some friends might shy away from even discussing some of these problems, simply because they are afraid of giving the wrong advice or prefer not to get drawn into the person's problems. It is the job of the outplacement counselor to help solve these very real problems.

A Positive Role for the Outplacement Counselor

With all of the above going on, it is important that the person carefully think through each of his moves. When the person gets into a situation that has him puzzled, rather than make a quick commitment, he would be better off asking for time to think it over. Unfortunately, most people engaged in the job search process do not have anyone with whom to work or plan their strategy. Thus, they are left to try to puzzle through the proper course of action on their own without being able to bounce their ideas off a more experienced person or have someone who is informed listen to them as they think through the pros and cons of each course of action that seems to be open to them.

Our sketch of the needs of the terminated executive should accomplish one thing. It should make the reader aware that once the termination interview has been completed, the problems for the person who has been let go are both substantial and only just beginning. As he gets further and further into the job search process, more and more decision points are reached.

To the extent that the job hunter makes amateurish mistakes or unfortunate decisions, the period of unemployment is extended unnecessarily. A decisive executive often flounders as he is confronted with the layers of decision making he has to go through during the job search process simply because he does not have an experience base upon which to draw in trying to sort through the correct answers. Continually, he reinvents the wheel. Outplacement counseling is a vehicle for helping the job hunter through this difficult period of adjustment.

9

Six Difficult
Termination Situations

TERMINATION IS SELDOM EASY. HOWEVER, some situations are more difficult to handle than others. We asked several outplacement consultants to identify the kinds of terminations that are especially difficult to handle. The following six problems emerged with an overwhelming degree of frequency. The experts we surveyed seemed especially sensitive to the problems managers have in dealing with these types of cases because they often receive requests for help in dealing with them.

Problem No. 1. The Long-Term Employee

When terminating someone, it somehow seems easier when the person is young and has only been with the company for a few years. However, if the person being let go has served 10, 15, or even 20-plus years with the organization, management feels an obligation to him or her and the manager doing the termination sometimes feels very guilty.

Consider the peculiarities that arise when terminating a long-term employee. First, the person has been out of the job market for a considerable length of time. He is very likely to suffer from a parochial viewpoint simply because he has spent such a long time with one company. He will have set ideas on how "things are done" and may be so in tune with the company's way that he will be at a distinct disadvantage in selling himself to other organizations. Second, his co-workers are likely to be especially sensitive to his treatment as a measure of the company's loyalty to its employees.

The first of these problems suggests that this person is especially in need of outplacement counseling after the termination interview. He is among the most likely to be susceptible to the pitfalls of the job search process, simply because he has been so far removed from it. Providing OPC services also helps to demonstrate to his colleagues that the company provided reasonable support to the person in recognition of his years of service to the organization.

Beyond providing OPC support the company should have a termination policy that recognizes longevity of employment as one of the criteria affecting the specifics of the support package. Generally, a long-term employee should receive generous financial and nonfinancial benefits, reflecting the problems of adjustment that confront him or her as well as the sense of obligation felt by the organization.

When terminating a long-term employee the company should use the same approach it uses with any other person. First, the manager must outline specifically what the employee has done to bring the situation to this point. Second, there should always be three concrete reasons the situation has come to such a conclusion. It should go without saying that efforts toward improving performance should have been exhausted prior to arriving at the termination decision.

When dealing with a long-term employee who is experiencing performance problems, it is imperative that his manager set specific performance criteria or objectives in an effort to turn the person's work around. Other employees will be sensitive to whether or not he received a fair shake when "push came to shove."

We have often observed a new manager, brought in to revive a poorly performing department, terminating people almost immediately without making a legitimate effort to allow them to improve their performance. Unfortunately, an opportunity for long-term employees to adjust to the new rules of the game is not provided. Almost always this is a mistake. A manager can, and should, set strict standards for subordinates and require almost immediate evidence of improved performance. However, the effort should be made to give people an opportunity to perform.

Nevertheless, when it becomes clear that the person is not going to improve, a straightforward termination must be made. With a long-term employee, one of the most cruel and psychologically damaging approaches is not to tell the person he is fired but have him sit in a kind of never-never land of half-truths.

It is equally damaging to give the person a series of minor tasks that are of little or no value to the organization. Both the employee and his associates perceive the lack of meaningful contribution the employee is being asked to make. Under such conditions, the empathy of close associates turns into ridicule. Worse, the person can lose confidence in his abilities or develop a bitterness that alters his character. Friends and colleagues begin avoiding him because of the unpleasantness of the situation.

When dealing with the long-term employee, it is best to terminate him as you would any other person, addressing the problem directly, using specific concrete reasons, and providing him with a substantial support package.

Problem No. 2. The Boss and Employee Are Good Friends

It would be easy to say that supervisors and employees should not be good friends because socializing and developing deep-rooted relationships can create long-term problems. In reality, managers frequently become attached to people and it becomes difficult to deal with them in a disciplinary way. At managerial levels, this frequently occurs as alliances are forged between executives. Long managerial working hours turn these alliances into a significant part of a manager's social circle.

Even when the person being dismissed is a close friend, one must be honest and state directly the reasons for the termination. To do less is to compromise the integrity of the organization. The real issue is somewhat direct, if difficult to accept. A manager has a responsibility to maintain the performance of an organization. When a subordinate is not performing or is violating some other aspect of employment criteria, not applying the same solution that would be applied in other cases violates the responsibility of the executive. Terminating the person may cost the manager his or her friendship, but the responsibility for doing so is clear.

To place the matter in perspective, corporate friendships are interrupted for other reasons. People change jobs or move to other divisions, and gradually the relationship fades. Termination is another aspect of the managerial environment that can affect personal relationships.

Although the above analysis seems cold, and no doubt will be cited someplace as an illustration of the fragility of relationships in corporate life, there is another side to it. Using a trumped-up rationale for letting a good friend sit and vegetate ultimately costs the manager in his dealings with others. Nothing undermines a manager's influence faster than a charge of favoritism; and perceptions of favoritism are difficult to control. Failure to terminate a close friend for cause compromises the manager's options in dealing with others.

When a manager finds himself facing the prospect of having to terminate a close friend, often his basic struggle is for some sense of reinforcement that he is doing the right thing. The emotional support of knowing that he has followed the guidelines of a solid corporate termination policy and that dismissal is the next step helps him over this difficult psychological hurdle. We have found, for example, that simply discussing the points covered above often places an executive's mind at ease. More than one person has said, "Of course I know you're right, but somehow I needed to talk it through anyway."

Problem No. 3. Members of Protected Classes

Minorities, women, and people over 40, of course, constitute a special risk for corporations discharging them. Unfortunately, this is true because most companies' performance appraisal systems are not adequate and managers do not coach people properly on what they are doing wrong.

Legislation prohibiting discrimination in employment practices dates back to the Civil Rights Act of 1964. This act established the Equal Opportunity Commission, which has the power to take companies to court if they are not in compliance. Essentially, Title VII of the Civil Rights Act makes discrimination illegal in all areas of the employment condition—hires, promotions, terminations, transfers, and layoffs.

Executive Order 11246, issued in September 1965, established the concept of affirmative action for government contractors. Essentially, affirmative action went beyond the requirement that corporations not discriminate; affirmative action mandated that companies doing business with the federal government take steps to eliminate patterns of past discrimination. Subsequent legislation further specified the protections accorded by EEO.

Contrary to the opinion of many managers, it is not virtually impossible to terminate a member of a protected class, although a company should be prepared to defend its decision. What is necessary is that the termination be made for "just business cause" and that the person have had previous knowledge that his work was not acceptable and yet did not improve. In short, EEO legislation requires that managers make sound, unbiased, and supportable business decisions, a requirement that makes many managers uncomfortable with regard to some of their personnel decisions.

Most of us are accustomed to having our biases go unchallenged when evaluating an employee. The problem is complicated by the failure to conduct and maintain sound performance reviews. As we have seen, historically courts have held that under common law an employer has the right to discharge an employee any time regardless of the reason. Thus, with the exception of those protected by union agreements, employees have pretty much been at the mercy of their bosses. EEO legislation has interrupted this condition as it applies to certain employees.

A combination of these factors has generated an overreaction on the part of many supervisors and managers—a fear of taking disciplinary action against an employee. This fear has been generated by a misunderstanding of what the law actually requires.

If the termination policies outlined in Chapter 3 and the disciplinary process in Chapter 4 are followed, there is no problem. Documentation that the employee has been told that his current performance is unacceptable should exist. Standards for improvement should have been communicated clearly at the time of these reviews. Finally, specific descriptive reasons for the termination should be given at the time of the firing. The support package should be consistent with what other employees of similar status within the organization have received. It is always good practice to review the case with the company's affirmative action specialist before taking action.

Of course, it is possible that the person will appeal the termination to the EEOC. However, if the termination is legitimate, the complaint will cost the company little other than the time of one of its personnel managers—certainly less than maintaining the problem employee. Many complaints never get past the preliminary investigation when it becomes clear that the company has acted in a thorough and aboveboard fashion.

In reality, the goal of corporate policy should be to afford all employees the protection EEO has provided certain classes: a thorough and documented review of actual performance. As far as federal and state laws are concerned, an employer is free to terminate any employee he or she wishes—provided such discipline is not motivated by a discriminatory purpose or handed out in a discriminatory manner. For example, an employer may not fire an employee who has complained of racial bias. Nor may an employer, faced with the need to lay off 25 out of 100 employees, lay off a disproportionate number of minority employees.

Terminations for a good cause, imposed in a consistent manner, without regard to race, religion, place of origin, sex, or age, are not unlawful. However, objective guidelines and their consistent application are very important elements in preventing claims of discrimination and in protecting the employer when claims are filed. Where an employer has no objective guidelines for imposing discipline, discrimination may be suspected.

For example, terminations should not be based on the subjective decisions of supervisors alone. Clear rules should be established, with corresponding penalties, and both should be made known and explained to employees. Then any violations should be recorded carefully. Terminating an employee for an unsatisfactory work record is lawful, but ample evidence should be compiled, recorded, and kept available. On the other hand, if a clear policy is instituted but the penalties are applied inconsistently, with a disparate effect on minorities, the employer will be found to have discriminated.

Also it is permissible to terminate a protected class employee for insubordination—refusing to obey reasonable work orders. It is important, however, that a claim of insubordination be supported by ample evidence and that there be no indication that a young, white male employee would not be treated in the same manner.

Absenteeism can also result in termination as long as the discharge is in accord with reasonable company rules applied to all workers. The same applies to the ability to perform work. Terminating a female employee because she is unable physically to perform her work is not necessarily sex discrimination merely because she is replaced by a male. On the other hand, replacing all female employees with males would probably amount to sex discrimination in the absence of evidence that the replaced females were individually unable to perform the work assigned to them.

Employers *are* prohibited from firing employees for reasons that have a disparate effect on minorities. For example, an employee may not be fired for having an arrest record or for having his salary garnisheed, unless the employer can prove a policy of such firings does not adversely affect minority employees. Therefore, in applying a personal conduct standard, three questions need to be answered.:

1. Will the policy have an adverse effect on minority employees?
2. If an adverse effect exists or will exist, is the standard necessarily related to job performance or warranted by some business necessity?
3. If there is a business necessity, is there an alternative with a lesser impact on minorities that will serve as well?

As the burden of proof on each of these questions will fall on the employer, a personal conduct standard must be closely thought through before it is instituted, and careful records and statistical information must be gathered and maintained if the standard is instituted. Once again, however, the regulations merely require that employers think through the business reasoning on which personnel policies are based.

Problem No. 4. The Person Who Overrates Himself or Herself

At times, a manager is confronted with terminating someone who not only fails to perceive how poor his performance has been, but seems to believe he is doing a superior job. Such a person is generally very resistant to efforts aimed at improving his perform- ance. Sessions a manager holds to attempt to correct his behavior turn into arguments during which the employee maintains his performance has been strong.

The reasons for such misconceptions can be complex. The manager has neither the training nor the resources to alter them significantly, and he shouldn't try. Regardless of how frustrating the situation becomes, the manager should stick to documenting the situation, clearly describing his expectations to the subordi- nate. When it is clear that the subordinate has repeatedly failed to meet those expectations, the manager should proceed with the termination procedure.

During the termination, the manager should avoid being ab- rupt, despite any show of bravado on the part of the employee. More than likely, he is quite terrified about the future. However, significant behavioral change will require professional counsel- ing. Thus, this person is a special candidate for outplacement counseling.

If the employee reacts with disbelief, the manager should support his position by referring to the missed performance standard. The theme of the manager's position should be "Maybe you'll do better elsewhere, but I believe you should examine your performance here carefully." The manager should encourage the person to discuss what he might do differently in the next job. This can help start the process of self-analysis, laying the ground- work for more effective outplacement counseling.

Above all, the manager should not compromise his position by suggesting that perhaps another boss might have seen things differently or adopting some similar posture. If the person's self-perception is ever to come more in line with reality, he will first have to admit his failures. Removing even part of his responsibility for his performance from his shoulders makes it too easy for him to rationalize away all his problems on the job.

Problem No. 5. The Employee with a Drinking Problem[1]

Alcoholism is a serious problem in our society, so serious that many corporations have begun to initiate programs to help their employees deal with it. It is, however, a difficult problem to get a person to admit. In fact, the employee often does not recognize that he has an alcohol problem. Often he attributes his abnormal drinking to other reasons. The disease, which is progressive over a period of ten to twenty years, usually becomes full-blown in people 45 to 55 years old. The individual is ordinarily powerless to stop this progression without assistance. Thus, a manager can be confronted with an employee who historically has been a good performer but with time has had his performance deteriorate drastically.

Once a manager feels fairly certain that an employee has a drinking problem, he or she must deal with it in a direct manner. Problem drinkers are not likely to admit to a problem; nor are they apt to be overly flustered when confronted with the issue. In most cases, they will be able to provide convincing excuses for their behavior.

In order to understand the nature of the problem, it must be recognized that alcoholics do not wish to change. One of the biggest favors a manager can do for someone with a drinking problem is to help him or her to see the negative repercussions of

[1]This discussion is extracted from John D. Drake, "Counseling Techniques for the Non-Personnel Executive" (New York: PEM, Drake Beam Morin, Inc., 1974). Used with permission.

the problem and the absolute need to get rehabilitation. Termination should be considered only when it is clear that the individual is not likely to deal with his problem, and that his performance is such that the organization can no longer tolerate the consequences.

A good way to begin a corrective counseling discussion in this area is for the manager to describe two or three instances in which he has observed poor behavior or job performance that caused him to believe a drinking problem exists. Having done that, he must then come down hard on the employee, indicating that unless the subordinate takes concrete steps to change, disciplinary action will be taken. The employee should be given a specific period of time to prove that he is taking effective steps to deal with his problem.

The manager can refer the individual to a corporate program or, if none is available, to Alcoholics Anonymous. AA will require that the employee himself call, but the manager can have the local number ready and give it to the employee.

In dealing with alcoholism, there is no easy middle ground. It cannot be overemphasized that a firm, direct step must be taken, and a manager must be prepared to follow through with disciplinary action if the employee does not seek help.

If efforts at getting the employee to deal with his problem fail after a period of time, and if the employee's performance continues to deteriorate, the manager is left with no alternative but to dismiss him. After that happens, the person who has lost his job is sometimes forced to face reality. This is especially likely to happen if supportive counseling is provided after the termination interview. Of course, such an outcome cannot be predicted.

At all times, the manager should remember that the employee is not being terminated for his drinking, but for lack of performance, and that should be the gist of the conversation. The reasons given should reflect the performance areas in which the individual has been informed that improvement must be made and which have failed to show any improvement.

In fact, this is the basic principle for dealing with any employee who has a personal problem that is interfering with the job, be it drugs, marital problems, or whatever. The manager should focus on specific performance problems. Avoid labeling the cause of the problem. After the employee has been warned repeatedly about the consequences of failing to deal with the performance problem and has made no effort at seeking outside help and the decision has been made that the company cannot continue to tolerate the situation, the actual termination is always for the performance problem, not for what is happening in the employee's personal life.

Problem No. 6. Group Terminations

One of the most difficult of managerial jobs is making the decision to reduce a company's workforce by a sizable percentage. Even more difficult is carrying out the staff reduction in an orderly fashion with a minimum amount of trauma for management, the organization in general, and the people being terminated.

Having worked with many of the nation's largest corporations in carrying out staff reductions, we have gained some particular insight into this challenge. Over the years, we have seen companies make catastrophic errors in their approach to staff reduction, but have seen other companies develop systematic programs and reduce work populations with a minimum of stress for everyone involved.

A Major Error

The primary error usually made when carrying out a staff reduction is hurrying the planning and organizing process. In essence, many companies decide to reduce their staffs and then order middle-level operating management to carry out the cuts immediately. Unfortunately, terminating large numbers of employees can have devastating effects on the organization for years to come.

As a rule of thumb, planning for a significant staff reduction should take upward of six months to a year. This means that when the possibility of staff reductions first appears, planning has to take place on a contingency basis. Companies that try to reduce their staffs by any significant amount with less planning run the gamut of the following problems:

- Class action suits
- Negative impact on internal morale
- Negative impact on corporate image in recruiting and maintaining managerial talent
- Negative impact on community or communities in which the corporation resides
- Poor national publicity
- Bad case of corporate conscience, which lingers on

Consider the following case. For the sake of anonymity, we will refer to the organization as Company X. This company had installed the latest cost-saving equipment, but still found its bottom line suffering from severe cost pressures. After some quick decisions, supported by a hastily completed study done by an outside consulting firm, top management decided on a 15 percent across-the-board reduction of exempt and nonexempt personnel in all departments.

Remember this point: Some departments were fat and others were lean. No guidelines were developed to handle the 15 percent. In addition, no guidelines were developed to identify who should be terminated. Some departments used pure seniority; others terminated for performance. Still others terminated purely at the discretion of the department manager.

To compound the problem further, management ordered the terminations to be initiated and completed within one month's time. Net result:

- Five class action suits, with a potential for many more

- A net 8.3 percent cut, missing bottom-line expectations.
- Morale at an all-time low
- An increase in the attrition rate of people they wanted to keep by 125 percent over the previous year
- Confusion as to corporate direction
- Lack of confidence in the organization by community leaders
- Bad public relations in general

Planning for Group Terminations

Problems like the ones experienced by the above company can be avoided through careful planning. In particular, several specific factors should be included in any group termination plan.

Determining target areas. When a company decides that a workforce reduction is necessary to preserve its economic viability, the first step in the planning process is identifying the areas in the organization that are to absorb staff reductions. The areas chosen should reflect the strategic plan of the organization.

Specific reduction goals should be set for each area of the company. The consequences of these reductions should be reviewed carefully by management and then, after any changes are made, commitment to the goals should be finalized by management.

The process for setting staff reduction goals should follow the same pattern of any effective planning effort. Priorities should be communicated downward, along with the underlying justification for concentrating cuts in some areas and not others.

Department heads should react to these proposals, giving their own reasoning for arguing for certain goal levels. Once these reactions have been reviewed and digested by senior management, specific goals should be made final and communicated downward. Division and department heads should then begin to establish implementation plans for reaching the goals.

Determining the basis for termination. Seniority, performance, and potential are the three most common guidelines for determining who, within a given job category, should be discharged. Seniority has the advantage of being totally objective; however, determining who goes and who stays solely on the basis of length of service doesn't always permit the organization to retain the best performers.

When performance becomes the key criterion used, management can retain the stronger performers. This approach is easier to implement when good performance appraisals have been maintained. If, as so often happens, everyone's annual appraisal indicates at least acceptable performance, decisions over who gets discharged take on a highly subjective flavor.

Retaining someone on the basis of his potential to the company is the most subjective of decisions. Assessing potential is always a speculative activity. Who is to say whether or not potential will be realized? Even measuring someone's potential is an elusive task, roughly akin to informed gambling. Still, there are times when consideration for someone's potential must enter into the retention decision.

At the exempt level of organizations, we recommend the use of performance as the primary criterion for identifying those who will be excluded from the cutback. This approach permits the organization to retain its best people. Seniority and potential can be used as a basis for retaining certain people under specific circumstances. Once all the above-average performers have been protected, seniority should become the dominant criterion.

This approach assumes satisfactory performance measures. If good performance reviews are not available, seniority emerges as the only justifiable criterion, with performance and potential only entering into isolated decisions.

Nonexempts, if not covered by a collective bargaining agreement, should be dealt with on the basis of seniority. The only exceptions should be people whose work has been rated as unacceptable. This approach is typically the fairest method for dealing with nonexempt employees.

Timing the terminations. Once the areas of the organization and the people who will be terminated have been designated, timing needs to be given consideration. In general, the timing should be early in the week. Once the first employees have been told, every effort should be made to complete the entire process as soon as possible. A week is generally too long. The uncertainty that runs through an organization once the process begins brings havoc to both people and the organization.

Those who are part of the cutback should be given at least two weeks' notice, along with severance pay at the final termination date. They will have an opportunity to get organized and the company will be demonstrating concern for them. Once everyone being discharged has been notified, an announcement to that effect should be made immediately.

Throughout the above process the company should not adopt what we call the avoidance syndrome. Since mass layoffs are so unpleasant, many companies try to act as if the cutback were not about to happen. If the grapevine starts to generate rumors of a staff reduction, the best approach is a direct one. Management should announce something similar to:

> "We hope to avoid a staff reduction, but given business conditions we are making contingency plans. No cutbacks will occur until (month/year)."

or

> "The company will have to reduce its staff by _____ percent. Complete plans have not been formulated, but no cutbacks will occur until (month/year)."

Honest answers to employee concerns allow management to remain in control of any employee misinformation and create considerable credibility once the cutback has been completed.

Group Outplacement Workshops

Increasingly, companies facing staff reductions are offering employees being discharged the opportunity of participating in a group outplacement workshop. These sessions are generally held one or two days after the termination interview and focus on job search skills. The following topics were included in group workshops for recent clients:

Exempt Employees

Day 1

Getting Organized
* Your attitude
* Planning your way to a new position
* How to react to family and friends
* The next steps

Career Guidance Survey
* Evaluation of the employee's interest patterns and how they relate to known occupational areas
* An opportunity to evaluate career paths

Life History Interview and Analysis of Experience
* Group exercises designed to assist the employee in identifying personal strengths from previous accomplishments

Day 2

Assistance in Approaching the Job Market
* The proper way to build a résumé
* Defining the contact network (one introduction is worth ten letters of inquiry)
* Target companies: defining goals
    Type of company

Size of company
Type of management
Financial status
Nature of product
What you "fit"

Day 3

The Interview (using closed-circuit TV)
- General pointers on how to be interviewed
- The tough questions
- The Drake Beam Morin rehearsal tape
- "Do I really want to live here?" (how to interview the boss)

Penetrating the "Defenses" of Target Companies
- Approaching the company
- Defining its needs and appealing to it
- Dealing with secretaries
- Tying down the interview

Negotiating Strategy
- How to tell if it is serious
- What to do if you have two offers
- Keeping your options open

Accepting an Offer
- Letter of confirmation
- Announcement of arrival

Nonexempt Employees

Day 1

Getting Organized
- Confidence rebuilding

- Reference building
- Financial security
- Self-determination
- Necessary groundwork

Approaching the Job Market
- Marketing strategy in the job hunt
- Marketing alternatives
- Personal contacts
- Newspaper advertisements
- Job application forms
- Employment agencies
- Corporations
- Unemployment bureaus
- State employment agencies

Day 2

Selling Yourself
- How to communicate more effectively
- Interviewing (using television as a training device)
- Interview feedback
- Reference validation

In conducting such workshops, it is best to strive toward having participants come from different organizational units. Otherwise people can waste valuable time on old grudges and complaints. Also, it is best to avoid extremes in organization levels. Senior employees may feel humiliated and lower-level employees may be intimidated. Ten to fifteen participants is the ideal size for a group outplacement workshop.

The beginning of these workshops is usually marked by skepticism and hostility. However, a skilled leader can gradually convert the group into a unit of people who are mutually supportive of each other. Participants come to see the content as helpful to them in their current situation. By the conclusion of the session, participants feel prepared to face a difficult and unpleasant situation. This feeling helps to sustain the morale of the organization they are leaving.

Index